The Guidebook of

ARMENIA

NATURE, HISTORY, CULTURE, RELIGION

Fourth edition, expanded

YEREVAN 2020

*Recommended by the Armenian Association
of Professional Tourist Guides*

ISBN 978–9939–0–1149–3

CONTENTS

Foreword..9

Facts About Armenia...10
Transport...11
Distance in km from Yerevan...11
Souvenirs..12
Several Armenian words with Latin transcription...13

History..15

The Origin 15
Eden...15
Hayasa..16
Hayk...17
Urartu..18
The Yervandyan (Yervanduni)...20
The Artaxid (Artashesyan)..23
Tigranes II 23
The last Artaxid..26
The Arsacid (Arshakuni)...27
The fall of the Arsacid 29
The Sasanid Armenia...29
Byzantine Armenia 30
Armenia under the Arab Caliphate..31
The Bagratid (Bagratuni)..32
The invasions of Seljuk Turks...32
Cilicia 33
Mongols in Armenia...34
The division of Armenia between the Ottoman Turkey and the Safavid Persia...........................35
The situation in Eastern Armenia (Persia) 37
The situation in Western Armenia...38
The Armenian Question 39
Abdul Hamid II massacres..40
The Young Turks..40
WWI and the Armenian Genocide 41
The first Republic of Armenia 42
The Soviet Armenia 45
Stalin regime...46
Armenia in the Great Patriotic War 47
Nikita Khrushchev: the leader of the Soviet Union 47
Leonid Brezhnev 48
Perestroika..49
Artsakh and Nagorno Karabakh conflict 49
Independent Republic of Artsakh 52
Economy 54
Nature...55
The Republic of Armenia 55
The Velvet Revolution...56
Population..57
Economy 60
Foreign policy..61
Armenian Diaspora..62
Armenia and the Silk Road..64
Christianity..67
Dogmas of the Armenian Apostolic Church 69
Sacraments 71
Hierarchy in the Armenian Church 72

Architecture 75
Khachkar 78
Climate Relief Nature Subsoil 79
Culture Language Alphabet Literature 91
Music 94
Miniature 95
Cochineal 96
Painting 96

The regions of Armenia and their places of interest 97

Shirak region 97
Marmashen Monastery 98
Artik 99
Haritchavank 99
Lmbatavank 100
Saint Sign (Surb Nshan) or Seven Wounds 100
Pemzashen 101
Yereruyk 101
Tavush region 102
Lastiver 103
Lake Parz 104
Little Armenian Switzerland 104
Mshkavank 105
Arakelots 105
Goshavank 106
Code of Laws 107
Haghartsin 109
Makaravank 112
Lori region 114
Stepanavan arboretum 115
Hnevank 115
Sanahin 116
Haghpat 118
Akhtala 121
Odzun 122
Kobayr 124
Khutchapi vank 124
Lori fortress 125
Ardvi 125
Sanahin bridge 126
The Molokons 126
Dsegh 127
Aragatsotn region 128
Amberd fortress 130
Yazidis 132
Hovhanavank 132
Saghmosavank 134
Aruch 135
Dashtadem 136
St. Katoghike of Talin 138
Oshakan 140
Mastara 141
Ararat region 142
Hovhannes–Karapet 143
Khosrov National Park 144
Artashat 144
Khor Virap 146
Kaqavaberd 147
Dvin 148

Armavir region...149
The Metsamor Museum 150
Sardarapat...151
Ejmiadzin..152
Hripsime 153
Zvartnots...154
Gayane 156
Gegharkunik region...157
Lake Sevan..158
Sevanavank..160
Noratus..162
Hayravank..163
Kotayk region 164
Tsaghkadzor ski resort 165
Geghard monastery 166
Garni temple...169
Havuts Tar 171
Kecharis 171
Vayots Dzor region..172
Areni 1 – Birds' Cave...174
Noravank monastery 176
Gladzor University...178
Smbataberd fortress 179
Jermuk 180
Zorats St. Astvatsatsin Church.....................................181
Selim Caravanserai..181
Syunik region...182
Relics Park of plane trees 183
Goris..183
Khndzoresk...183
Tatev..187
Wings of Tatev..189
Zorats Karer (Karahunj) 190
Vorotnavank 192
Places of interest in Artsakh...194
Gandzasar..195
Tigranakert...196
Dadivank..197
Ghazanchetsots...198
Shushi..198
Askeran (Mayraberd)...199
Amaras...200
Plane tree in Skhtorashen 200
Umbrellas (Mamrot kar)...201
Yerevan..202
Gastronomy 210
Several Armenian dishes 211

Parables...212
The lazy daughter–in–law 212
The king 212

Legends 213
The legend of lavash 213
The legend of duduk 213
Vardavar 214

USEFUL INFORMATION...218
Yerevan museums..218

YEGHISHE CHARENTS

I Love My Sweet Armenia's...
I love my sweet Armenia's word which is filled with the taste of sun,
I love our old lyre's melody from its mournful and weeping strings,
The vivacious fragrance of the blood–like flowers and the roses,
I love as well the graceful and agile dance of Nayirian girls.

I love as well our gloomy sky, our pure waters, luminous lake,
The summer's sun and the winter's sublime wind with a dragon's voice,
Also the black, unwelcoming walls of the huts lost in the dark,
And I love the thousand–year stone of the ancient cities as well.

No matter where I am yet I shall not forget our mournful songs,
Shall not forget our steel–lettered books which now have become prayers,
No matter how sharply they pierce my heart our wounds so soaked with blood,
Even then I love my orphaned and my bloodied, dear Armenia.

For my longing heart there is not, not even one another tale,
There's no brighter forehead than that of Kouchag and Naregatsi,
Pass the whole world, there's no summit as white as that of Ararat,
Like glory road, unreachable, I love as well my Mount Massis.

Translated by Shant Norashkharian

Ես իմ անուշ Հայաստանի արևահամ բառն եմ սիրում,
Մեր հին սազի ողբանվագ, լացակումած լարն եմ սիրում,
Արնանման ծաղիկների ու վարդերի բույրը վառման,
Ու նաիրյան աղջիկների հեզաճկուն պարն եմ սիրում:

Սիրում եմ մեր երկինքը մուգ, ջրերը ջինջ, լիճը լուսե,
Արևն ամռան ու ձմռվա վիշապաձայն բուքը վսեմ,
Մթում կորած խրճիթների անյուրընկալ պատերը սև
Ու հնամյա քաղաքների հազարամյա քարն եմ սիրում:

Ու՛ր էլ լինեմ – չեմ մոռանա ես ողբաձայն երգերը մեր,
Չեմ մոռանա աղոթք դարձած երկաթագիր գրքերը մեր,
Ինչքան էլ սուր սիրտս խոցեն արյունաքամ վերքերը մեր –
էլի՛ ես որբ ու արնավառ իմ Հայաստան-յա՛րն եմ սիրում:

Իմ կարոտած սրտի համար ո՛չ մի ուրիշ հեքիաթ չկա,
Նարեկացու, Քուչակի պես լուսապսակ ճակատ չկա.
Աշխա՛րհն անցի՛ր, Արարատի նման ճերմակ գագաթ չկա,
Ինչպես անմահ փառքի ճամփա՝ ես իմ Մասիս սա՛րն եմ սիրում:

Statue of Sasuntsi Davit (David of Sasun), the main hero of Armenia's national epic poem "Daredevils of Sasun"

Foreword

In this guidebook we've tried to briefly present our country in historical and cultural numbers and facts simply hoping that you may find a small corner in your heart for Armenia. And if one day you decide to visit it, let us welcome you...

Being one of the oldest nations in the world, nowadays Armenians possess a small territory in high and mighty mountains of Southern Transcaucasia.

The series of vicissitudes that this land has experienced during the course of its history due to its inconvenient geographic situation is just unbelievable. Nevertheless, thanks to it the nation learnt to fight, resist, and protect its culture, religion, language and national identity.

Some people consider Armenians of special interest for being the first Christian nation, others - for having survived the Genocide organized by the Government of the Young Turks. There are persons, who are interested in Armenia, because it was one of the fifteen Republics of the former Soviet Union, while others are amazed by the courage and the values demonstrated by Armenians during the war for the independence of Nagorno Karabakh.

Finally, the incomparable desire to live in their Motherland is simply impressive; even when obliged to leave their land and after changing many generations, Armenians "abroad" are still full of surprising Armenian nostalgia; they continue supporting their "owns", forming a strong and solid rearguard called Armenian Diaspora.

The Armenian society is open, but at the same time very conservative and traditional. Having the family as the core of the society, people here follow the patterns formed within the family; the traditional patterns, which consist of respecting the old and the children, go in line with an ancient Armenian proverb: "The water for the child, the word for the old".

The guest has a very special place in any house; even in a very poor family the guest would never notice or be aware about the host's difficulties and problems, because of possessing a certain sense of pride typical for the nations of the Caucasus.

The modern Armenian reality is a difficult transition from the Soviet regime to capitalism, the process of overcoming the consequences of the war, economic blockade, the power to erase the traces of the Soviet bureaucratic heritage, as well as the astounding vitality of the Armenian nation and its will to create a dignified future.

Facts About Armenia

Official Name:	Hayastan
Location:	Asia, Transcaucasia
Northern latitude:	between 38° – 42°
Eastern latitude:	between 43° – 47°
Neighboring countries:	Georgia, Iran, Turkey and Azerbaijan
Form of Government:	Republic
Founded:	IV - II centuries BC
Independence Day:	28 May, 1918, 21 September 1991 (from the USSR)
Capital:	Yerevan (1 122 000 inhabitants)
Area:	29 743 km²
Population:	2 998 600 (according to 2016 census)
Ethnic groups:	Armenians 97.9%, Yazidis 1.3%, Russians 0.5%, Assyrians 0.1%
Religion:	Apostolic Christians 93.6%, Yazidizm practitioners 1.3 %, Orthodox Christians 0.5%, Catholic Christians 0.4%
Official language:	Armenian
Major cities:	Yerevan, Gyumri, Vanadzor
Literacy:	99.4 %
Currency:	Armenian Dram (AMD, code 051)
Climate:	continental (cold winter and hot summer)
Average temperature:	Plain: January – 5, July + 25 Mountains: January –10, July +20
Average altitude:	1700-1800 m
Electricity:	220 V (50 Hz)
Plug type:	C, F
Internet domain:	.am
Time zone:	UTC +4
In summer	UTC +5
Telephone code:	+374
Holidays:	January 1–7, January 28, March 8, April 24, May 1, May 9, May 28, July 5, September 21.
Timetables:	from Tuesday to Sunday (except Matenadaran: from Tuesday to Saturday), the majority is open 10:00–17:00 (Except the History Museum and National Art Gallery of Armenia 11:00–18:00, on Sundays 11:00–17:00, the Genocide Museum 11:00–16:00)
Museums:	from Tuesday to Sunday (except Matenadaran: from Tuesday to Saturday), the majority is open 10:00–17:00 (except the History Museum and National Art Gallery 11:00–18:00, on Sundays 11:00–17:00, the Genocide Museum 11:00–16:00)
Shops:	In big cities there are 24–hour supermarkets. The trade centers operate 10:00–19:00.
Souvenir shops:	10:00–20:00 (11:00–21:00) without holidays The craftsmanship market, Vernissage, is open on Saturdays and Sundays 10:00–18:00 (there can also be some stands open during the working days of the week).

The country is very safe and secure; nevertheless, it is advised to be careful with the traffic, as the traffic rules are not always followed.

Transport

"Zvartnots" International Airport is located 10 km away from the capital. Since autumn 2011 new terminals started operating. No taxes are paid at the departure. At the airport exit one can use taxi services; it takes about 12 Euros to get to the city center. Within the city the taxi fee is much cheaper: 1 km equals to 0.2 Euros.

There is also a metro in Yerevan, which has a line of only 10 stations. The closest station to the center is situated on Nalbandyan Street next to the Republic Square. From the public transport one may use buses and minibuses. The fee equals to 0.2 Euros. In Yerevan there are two interregional stations: in the North (Tbilisi freeway) and the central one (Admiral Isakov Avenue). There are also trolleybuses in the capital. Because of the economic blockade the railway operates only in the direction of Georgia. The railway station in Yerevan is located in David of Sasun Square next to David of Sasun metro station.

Cable cars (ropeway) function in the health resorts of Tsaghkadzor, Jermuk, at Tatev Monastery.

Note: Dear traveler,

Due to the fact that the roads do not have good signposting, are not always in proper condition or the majority of them are mountainous, it is recommended to request services of a local driver in case of renting a car. Another option would be hitchhiking; the country is safe and secure for doing it. Not all historical monuments have a car access; please make sure to clarify it before your travel there.

Distance in km from Yerevan

Abovyan – 16	Berd – 186	Kapan – 320	Stepanavan – 139
Akhtala – 186	Chambarak – 125	Maralik – 105	Talin – 74
Akhuryan – 126	Charentsavan – 36	Martuni – 130	Tashir – 162
Alaverdi – 162	Dilijan – 96	Masis – 14	Tsaghkadzor – 55
Aparan – 59	Ejmiadzin – 20	Meghri – 393	Tumanyan – 148
Ararat – 47	Gavar – 98	Meghrut – 149	Vanadzor – 115
Armavir – 48	Geghard – 31	Noyemberyan – 185	Vardenis – 168
Artashat – 30	Goris – 236	Sevan – 66	Vayk – 139
Artik – 105	Gyumri – 126	Shamlugh – 196	Vedi – 49
Ashotsk – 165	Hrazdan – 50	Sisian – 217	Yeghegnadzor – 122
Ashtarak – 22	Ijevan – 131	Spitak – 95	Yeghvard – 30
Ayrum – 205	Jermuk – 178	Stepanakert – 351	

Souvenirs

The souvenirs can be acquired in the specialized shops, as well as in "Vernissage", which is an open–air handicraft street market and is open only during the weekend from 10:00–18:00. The market is situated in Hanrapetutyan and Khanjyan streets close to the Republic Square. Normally the craftsmen themselves tend to sell their products. It is also possible to bargain, but you may receive up to 10% reduction as a maximum. In the market they sell typical Armenian craftsmanship; carved wood (small cross stones, plates, vases, backgammon), precious and semi-precious stones (obsidian, malachite, amber, agate, jasper), jewelry from those stones, ancient and new carpets, silver jewelry, T–shirts and hats; waistcoats, caps, bags made of a national dress fabric, silk scarves, handkerchiefs etc. One can find almost the same variety in the souvenir shops.

One of the best souvenirs to get from Armenia is the Armenian brandy. All kind of trade is performed in local currency, AMD, except for the street markets. There are exchange posts in big supermarkets, banks and hotels. To get informed about the cultural events it is recommended to consult the notice board close to the building of Opera House and Philharmonic Hall.

Several Armenian words with Latin transcription

Thanks – shnorakalutyun – շնորհակալություն

Hello! Good afternoon – barev dzez, bari or, good morning – bari luys – բարի օր, բարև ձեզ, բարի լույս

See you *(later)*– tstesutyun – ցտեսություն

How are you? – inchpes es? – Ինչպես ես

Fine, Ok – lav – լավ

Bad – vat – վատ

Yes – ayo *(ha)* – Այո *(հա)*

No – voch *(che)* – Ոչ *(չէ)*

I love – Yes sirum em – Ես սիրում եմ

I want – Yes uzum em – Ես ուզում եմ

I like – Indz dur e galis – Ինձ դուր է գալիս

How much does it cost? – Inch arje *(j like ¨Jean¨ in French)* – Ի՞նչ արժե

This is tasty– Hamegh e – Համեղ է

Please – Khndrem – Խնդրեմ

You are welcome, not at all – Charje *(j like ¨Jean¨ in French)* – Չարժե

Where is… ? Vortegh e gtnvum – Որտե՞ղ է գտնվում

Coffee – surch – սուրճ

Beer – garejur *(j like ¨John¨ in English)* – գարեջուր

Wine – gini – գինի

OK – Yeghav – Եղավ

The Armenian bread "lavash", included in UNESCO intangible heritage list

HISTORY

The Origin

The Armenian nation comes from and continues its development in the Armenian Plateau, which being the cradle of the nation, occupies a bit more than 400 thousand km². In the North the territory of the Armenian Plateau reaches the Lesser Caucasus mountain range, in the South the Armenian Taurus mountains, in the West it comes to the Euphrates valley and in the East gets to the Pre–Caspian valley. The central part consists of a broad high plateau with valleys and rugged mountains. Almost in the center stands the Biblical Mount Ararat (currently in the Turkish territory) with its two peaks: Lesser Ararat (Sis, 3925 m) and Greater Ararat (Masis, 5165 m). To the west from the mountain lies the Armenian mountain range Par. The mountain range of Lesser Caucasus is formed of a series of mountains, among which Aragats (4090 m), the highest peak of the contemporary Armenia, stands out. Similar to the Biblical mountain, it is also an inactive volcano. In this very plateau in the second millennium

Armenia, sight from space

BC started the formation of the Armenian nation, which lasted for almost thousand years. Various tribes that lived in the plateau and commanded diverse languages participated in the formation process. Nevertheless, two big Armenian -speaking tribes, "the hays" and "the Armens" played the most crucial role in it; their gradual unification with th rest of the tribes gave birth to the Armenian nation. The neighboring countries and nations also had an impact on this complex formation process.

Eden

Some parts of Armenia, especially the valley of Araks and the region of Van, are one of the most extraordinary sites of beauty and fertility. This has led to support a theory that the Garden of Eden, mentioned in the Bible, was located in Armenia. Certainly, one should state that the legend, according to which Noah's Ark landed on the Mount Ararat, has a certain historical justification of a symbolic character, as a huge variety of animals, birds and plants, including the vines (according to the legend planted by Noah), developed from the species that

Lesser Ararat and Greater Ararat (Sis and Masis) and the valley of Ararat

still exist in Armenia and in the Caucasus. Nevertheless, only 1/4 of the territory of Armenia can be qualified as "the land of milk and honey". An important part of the mountainous area of Armenia is practically uninhabitable, except for being used by the nomadic shepherds, who look for summer pasture for their herd.

Hayasa

The first proto-Armenian state formations originated in the western part of the plateau in the valley of the Euphrates next to the state known as Hayasa which extended in the north-western part of the Armenian Highland. Hayasa kingdom received its name from hays tribes. Its population was mainly engaged in agriculture and stockbreeding. Hayasa kingdom had borders with the Hittits, who were the main enemy, and only in the beginning of the XIV century BC invaded the country twice. However, their invasion failed due to the strong resistance they received; the fight ended in signing a peace treaty, which was afterwards violated by the new prince of Hayasa.

Other Armenian–speaking tribes were located on the rest of plateau's territory. South from Hayasa there was the country of Sukhmu (the name of the inhabitants was the same). Its name coincides with the name "somekhi", which is the way Georgians call Armenians. More to the south, on the right bank of the river Euphrates, the Tegarama country was situated, mentioned in the Bible as the house of Torgom (Togarma). South from

■ *Hayasa Western Asia (II m BC)*

Tegarama was Melid country, with its two neighbors, Hate and Tsopk. Southwest of the plateau there were the principalities of Arme and Urme, comprised predominantly of Armenian tribes. The latter were mentioned in the references of the V century BC famous Greek historian Herodotus. The territory between the river Euphrates and lake Van was occupied by the tribal confederation called Nairi ("the land of rivers" in Assyrian), which incorporated various Armenian tribes and was often subjected to Assyrian invasions.

Hayk

The monument of Hayk the Patriarch (Sculptor A. Nurijanyan)

Coming back to the tradition and Biblical version; according to the genealogy of Movses Khorenatsi (Armenian historian from the IV century), Hayk was Noah's great–great grandson; Khafet–Gamer–Tiras–Torgom–Hayk (from the race and house of Torgom). After the dispersion and confusion of the humanity with regard to the failure of Babel construction, the titan Bel used the opportunity to seize the power. But Hayk refused to obey him; after having his son Aramaneak in Babylonia, he left for the North towards the country of Ararat together with his sons and daughters, grandsons, around 300 strong men and with all his domestic animals. He got established on the slope of the mountain, in the plain already inhabited by a small number of people, who were previously dispersed. Hayk took them under his domination. The population, living in the south of the plain, voluntarily obeyed the titan. When the titan Bel extended his reign over everyone, he sent one of his sons with several faithful people to the North to tell Hayk to obey him in order to live in peace. Hayk sent the messengers back with a very severe answer. Bel mobilized a large army with an infantry and advanced to the country of Ararat. The confrontation between the two giants terminated with the death of Bel in Hayks' arms. Hayk dominated the country (currently the name of the country sounds like "Hayastan"). With regard to the origin of the Armenian nation, the supporters of various opinions share the idea that as a nation Armenians were formed in II and I millenniums BC and the formation took place in the Armenian Highlands. This factor, namely the geographic situation, has left its traces during the whole course of the history. Being situated in the crossroad of the Western and Eastern civilizations, from the ancient times it has known both European and Asian cultures. Because of this same geographic situation the Armenian Plateau was continuously subjected to multiple invasions of the Westerners heading to the East and, more frequently, in the opposite direction. The latter predestined the peculiarities of the historical path that Armenia went through. The geographical factor is still relevant even in our days.

Urartu

The formation of the Armenian nation during one of the phases of its history coincides with the existence of one of the strongest ancient kingdoms of the East, the kingdom of Ararat (Urartu state). The heart of Urartu and ancient Armenia is centered around lake Van,

Chronicle on top of the rock in Van

in the middle of the Araks river valley, on the mountain Ararat and on the upper course of the Tigris and the Euphrates rivers. Being born of a tribal confederation in the North of Assyria, very soon Urartu established itself as an independent state. An alliance against the common enemy, the Assyrians, was quickly set up among the sovereigns of Urartu and the kings of Mitanni. The same alliance during the harsh times would allow the Hurrians (especially Mitanni people) to escape the Assyrian power and find refuge in Urartian mountains. When the Assyrians were liberated from the Aramaics, they launched campaigns against Urartu, including a raid against the capital (865 BC). In fact, the recognition of Urartu kingdom by Assyria is an unequivocal sign that the country of the North was converting into an enemy to be careful with. The confrontations between Urartians and Assyrians continued during the following century and a half with changing luck for both sides.

The development of Urartu reached its crucial point during the IX and VIII centuries BC turning it into a state that dominated extensive territories around lakes Van and Urmia, united around the well–established capital in Thuspa (Van). The trade was flowing without any problem in all directions. Contacts were established with the confederation set up in the North between the Taochi, Qolha or Colchi. With the aim of regional development Urartians referred to deportations in order to widen up the cultivable areas. Among the main export products were metal tools, horses, wine, wheat and barley. To cultivate the soil, Urartians turned into a great example of fluvial work constructors; the channels, artificial lakes, water tanks allowed to supply water into its cities and towns, (it is worth mentioning that the plumbing system built by the Urartian king Menua still supplies water to Van city and its surrounding), at the same time to provide water for the fields of wheat, barley, rye and spelt.

In the half of the VIII century BC Urartu demonstrated its military rise by the means of destruction and domination of the Taochi and confrontations with the country of Colchi. Those kinds of incursions gave an access to the coast of the Black Sea and thus increased the trade route, which originating from Susa was then passing through Urartu and ending in Trebizond. Around 720 BC a flow of people coming from the North, the Cimmerians and the Scythians, and afterwards the expansion of Iranians from the South (Medes and Neo–Babylonians) created disturbances and change in Asia Minor, in consequence Urartu

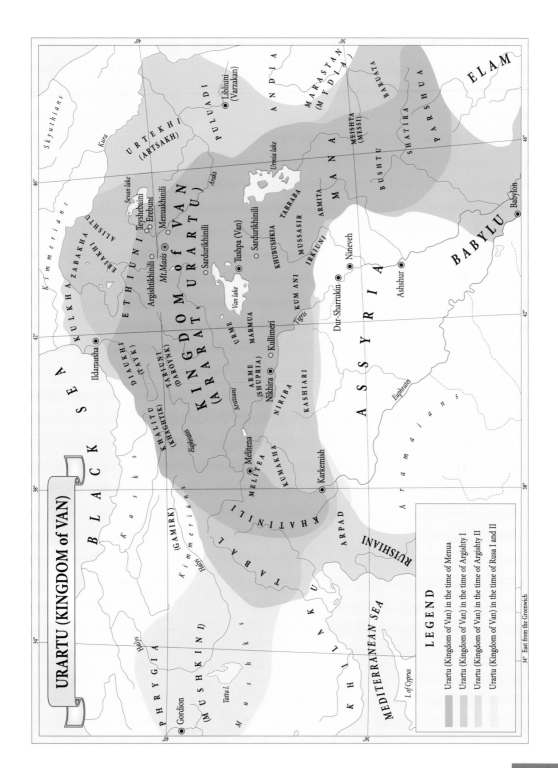

URARTU (KINGDOM of VAN)

BLACK SEA

MEDITERRANEAN SEA

I. of Cyprus

ELAM

BABYLU

ASSYRIA

MANA

LEGEND

Urartu (Kingdom of Van) in the time of Menua

Urartu (Kingdom of Van) in the time of Argishty I

Urartu (Kingdom of Van) in the time of Argishty II

Urartu (Kingdom of Van) in the time of Rusa I and II

34° East from the Greenwich

Cuneiform inscription Argishti I (782 BC)

Sculpture of a mythological creature, found in Erebuni (Arin Berd)

as well as Assyria began to weaken. The opportunity was wisely grasped by the nation that participated in the destruction of Hittite Empire and later seized the power vacuum in the Asia Minor left by the extinction of the aforementioned country. The invaders got established in Urartu most probably during the era, when Assyria was already collapsing under the armies of Medes and Babylonians.

Finally, Urartu fell in the beginning of the VI century BC under the attacks of the invaders from the North, Cimmerians and Scythians, and effectually under the pressure of the Medes from Persia. Many tribes were the part of Urartu state, among which the Armenian tribes presented the majority. Within Urartu the Armenian tribes not only preserved their identity, but also succeeded in "armenizing" several other regions and tribes. The Armenian tribes were the most resistant ones among those that formed the part of Ararat country and were the direct inheritors of the Urartian state, forming their own country after the collapse of the kingdom.

The Yervandyan (Yervanduni)

The first references about Armenia being independent date back to VII century BC. According to these sources, Armenians took part in the wars against Assyrians fighting together with two ally countries: Babylonia and Media (612 BC). As the old tradition states, the Armenian leader Paruyr, in return to supporting his allies, was recognized by them as the king of Armenians. A new Armenian dynastywas quickly formed in the capital of Ararat kingdom, Tushpa–Van. The dynasty was established by one of the relatives of Paruyr, Yervand Sakavakyac. In accordance with his name, the dynasty was called the Yervandyan (Yervandites). The Yervandyan succeeded in uniting the Armenian Highlands, the population of which was already Armenian speaking, and established the first Armenian state. Armenia

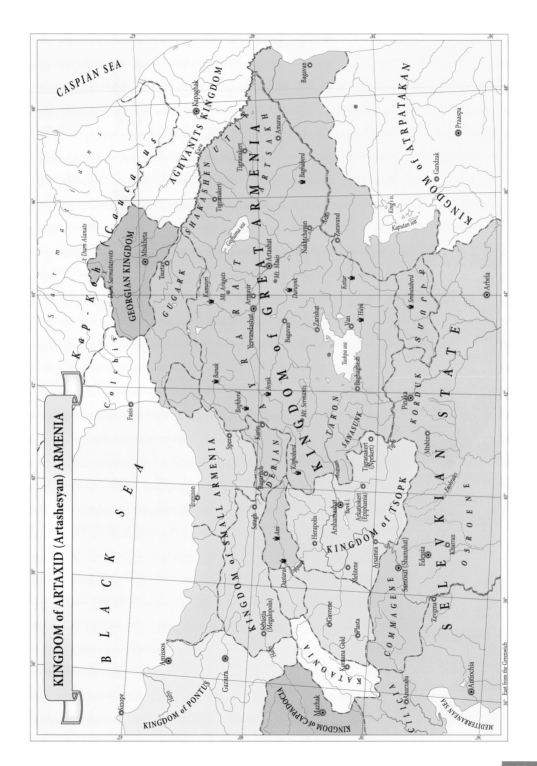

KINGDOM of ARTAXID (Artashesyan) ARMENIA

CASPIAN SEA

BLACK SEA

MEDITERRANEAN SEA

GEORGIAN KINGDOM

AGHVANITS KINGDOM

GREAT ARMENIA

KINGDOM of ATRPATAKAN

KINGDOM of SMALL ARMENIA

KINGDOM of PONTUS

KINGDOM of CAPPADOCIA

KINGDOM of TSOPK

COMMAGENE

SELEVKIAN STATE

OSROENE

CILICIA

KATAONIA

KINGDOM of TARON

KATARK

SANASUNK

KORDUK

SUNIK

ARTSAKH

UTIK

SHAKASHEN

GUGARK

AYRARAT

DERJAN

Caspian sea

Kaputan sea

Tiokhpa sea

Sevania sea

King's is.

Kap - Koh / Caucasus

Sarmatians

Colchis

■ *Battle of Gaugamela*

■ *The coin of Yervand II*

managed to maintain its independence and soon acquired a powerful ally, Cyrus the Great, who rose against Media. At the end he defeated Media being supported by the Armenian king Tigran I. In 550 BC Cyrus established the Achaemenid Persian Empire (the biggest of the era), where Armenia had a privileged place until Darius I came to the throne. He was the one, who called the Armenian country Armenia and its inhabitants Armenians in the Behistun Inscription. Almost two centuries Armenia was one of the satrapies under the Achaemenid Persia. However, the satraps were Armenians from the Yervandyan dynasty. In the last decade of Achaemenid Empire Armenia was divided into two parts: Armenia Major (Hayk Major) and Lesser Armenia (Hayk Minor).

The situation changed with the invasion of Alexander the Great at the end of the IV century BC. A new period started with his invasions into the Western Asia: the Hellenistic era. Since Alexander's troops did not enter the Armenian territory it got its independence back.

The enormous empire, created by Alexander, got divided into several parts after his death (323 BC). The largest one among them was the Seleucids, which posed a serious threat to neighboring Armenia. In 201 BC the troops of the Seleucid king Antiochus III defeated the Armenian Yervandyan dynasty. However, this situation lasted for only ten years, as Antiochus himself was defeated by the Roman troops and his empire began collapsing. Two Armenian leaders, Artashes and Zareh, who were previously leading the Seleucid army, allied with the Romans and were declared the independent kings of Hayk Major and Tsopk respectively.

The Artaxid (Artashesyan)

Artashes I (189–160 BC), being one of the most powerful kings in the Armenian history, was also the founder of the new royal Artaxid dynasty. Artashes I (Artaxias), using the politics of uniting small Armenian kingdoms around Hayk Major, considerably widened the frontiers of his kingdom. According to the chroniclers of that era in the North he reached the valley of the Kura river, in the South he got to the Tigris river, in the East to the Caspian Sea and to the river Euphrates in the West. Of upmost importance was the fact that the extended country was nationally homogeneous and the whole population was speaking the same language: Armenian. The same king carried out a series of agrarian, military and administrative reforms. He founded the capital of Artashat in the valley of Ararat, as well as other cities.

Tigranes II

Hayk Major (Greater Armenia) reached the apogee of its power during the reign of Tigranes (Tigran) II the Great (95–55 BC), the grandson of Artashes I and the most prominent general and politician of the Artaxid dynasty. During the first decades of his rule Tigranes II carried out a lot of conquests, as a result of which the Armenian kingdom expanded beyond its traditional boundaries. Tigranes the Great united a series of countries with Armenia in the South and Southeast (Atropatene and Mesopotamia from the North) and in the West and Southwest (Syria, Phoenicia, Commagene, Cilicia). Tsopk, the last independent Armenian kingdom, was also among the conquered countries.

Neither the Seleucid kingdom, which was in its decline era, nor the Parthian state, was able to resist the conquests of the consolidated Armenian kingdom. The head of the Parthian state was even forced to refuse his traditional title of "the king of the kings" in favor of the Armenian

Tigranakert Fortress

■ *Tigranes the Great (Painter Fuzaro, 1885)*

king Tigranes II. The Armenian territory grew almost three times as big turning into one of the most influential powers. Its borders stretched from the Caspian to the Black Seas ("from sea to sea Armenia"). During the early years of his reign the capital city of Armenia was the city Artashat, then for a short period of time Tigranes the Great converted Antioch, one of the largest cultural centers of the ancient East, into a capital until the construction of the new capital, Tigranakert in the 80s BC.

Carrying out the conquests, Tigranes II allied with the king of Pontus Mithridates Eupator. The alliance was further strengthened by the marriage of Tigranes and Cleopatra, the daughter of Mithridates. During the epoch, when Tigranes was making his invasions, Pontus had already fought various times against the Romans, who were trying to conquer new territories in the Asia Minor. Both sides fought with mixed success; the situation altered, when Rome sent one of its greatest generals, Lucius Lucullus, against Mithridates. In a series of battles the Romans defeated Mithridates and conquered Pontus. Mithridates, already having lost his

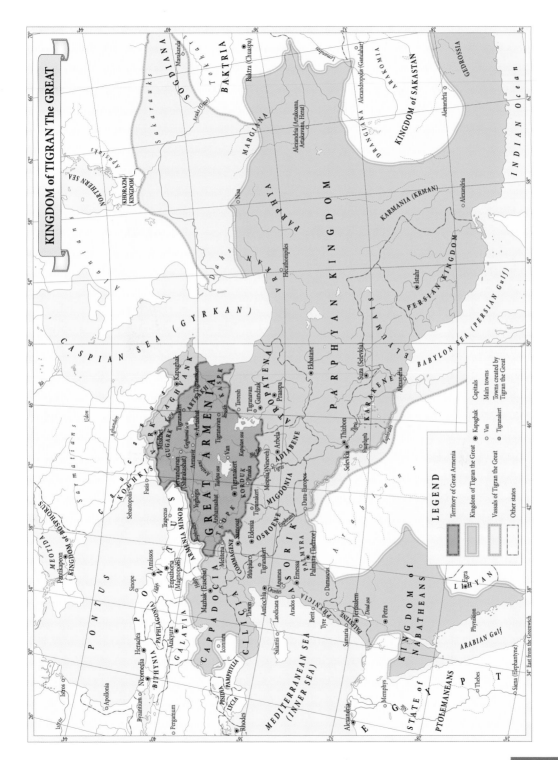

KINGDOM of TIGRAN The GREAT

LEGEND

Territory of Great Armenia
Kingdom of Tigran the Great
Vassals of Tigran the Great
Other states

Kapaghak — Capitals
Van — Main towns
Tigranakert — Towns created by Tigran the Great

● Kapaghak
○ Van
● Tigranakert

kingdom, found a refuge in Armenia having his son–in–law and ally Tigranes there. This prepared a ground for a confrontation between Rome and Armenia. In 69 BC Lucullus led his troops towards Tigranakert; they defeated the Armenian army, occupied the capital, plundered and destroyed it afterwards. After gaining the first victory, Lucullus decided to invade the second capital of Armenia, Artashat. However, the expedition of the Roman army inside the country failed. The Romans started retrieving; Tigranes and Mithridates persecuted them and managed to liberate the country from the enemy.

The Roman Republic could not accept the defeat. The General Pompeius took over the dismissed Lucullus and led the Roman army. Very soon he defeated Mithridates and invaded Armenia, addressing the main attack towards Artashat.

Seeing the superiority of the Roman power, Tigranes II agreed to sign a treaty in 66 BC in Artashat. According to the treaty Armenia was losing all conquered territories and was obliged to pay huge military fines. Nevertheless, the treaty of Artashat was Tigranes' diplomatic victory; he maintained the independence and the territorial integrity of Hayk Major. Rome was not interested in having Armenia as an enemy in the prospective war against Parthia. Consequently, it was mentioned in the treaty that Armenia is "the ally and the friend of the Roman nation". The last decade of the reign of Tigranes II was peaceful and calm for Armenia. The powerful king passed away in 55 BC.

The emerged Roman–Parthian confrontation created a new political reality for Armenia, which lasted for several centuries despite the fact that the countries involved in these relations around Armenia were changing. First and foremost, Armenia had to worry about its own independence and territorial integrity.

The last Artaxid

During the first years of the reign of son and heir of Tigranes II, Artavasdes II (55–35 BC), the Romans organized an expedition towards Parthia, sending there an army led by the General Marcus Crassus. Taking into consideration the existing politico–military situation, Artavasdes II allied with Parthia. The invasion of Crassus ended up with Romans' defeat. Crassus was assassinated in 53 BC. In 36 BC Rome organized the second expedition against the Parthian state. The head of the Roman troops was Marco Antonio. The Roman army was

Coin of Artavasdes II

moving towards Parthia through the southern regions of Armenia. This automatically involved Armenia in the war and forced Artavasdes to give some of his troops to Romans. However, after the first Roman defeat, the Armenian king immediately withdrew the troops. Losing a considerable part of his army and being forced to step back, Antonio accused the Armenian king in conspiracy and declared him an accomplice of the Roman defeat organized by the Parthians. It did not take too much time for Antonio to send various invitations to Artavasdes under the pretext of consulting about the new expeditions towards Parthia, as well as discussing the marriage of Artavasdes' daughter and Antonio's son. The Armenian king, perfectly realizing that it was a trap, rejected those invitations. Ultimately, Antonio entered Armenia, reached Artashat and Artavasdes had to surrender. He and his family, being chained, were taken to Alexandria (Egypt), where according to the order of Antonio's wife, Cleopatra, Artavasdes was executed, after having passed several years in prison, for refusing to praise the beauty of the queen Cleopatra.

During the following decades the last representatives of the Artaxid dynasty, who were protected sometimes by Rome, at other times by Parthia, occupied the Armenian throne. In the I century BC the Artaxid dynasty came to its end.

The Arsacid (Arshakuni)

The old Armenian state was in a serious crisis. In the first half of the I century the kings, appointed by Rome, successively reigned in Armenia. Amicable relationship was established between the kings of Parthia and Armenia. In 52 the king of Parthia Vologases (Vagharsh I) and his brother Tiridates entered Armenia and occupied Artashat and Tigranakert. Relying on the Armenian support, Tiridates proclaimed himself the king of Armenia. Since then the long fight between the Roman and Armenian–Parthian legions started. The new emperor, Neron, sent the General Corbulo to the eastern provinces with an aim to resolve the issue related to the succession of throne in Armenia. In 58 the operation started; he attacked the king of Armenia, Tiridates I. Under his order the legions captured the cities of Artashat and Tigranakert.

In 62 Neron sent Roman legions against Armenia again. This time, before coming to the battlefield, the Roman troops got surrounded by the Armenian–Parthian army and had to surrender. After these events Neron was forced to accept his defeat; the Armenian king Tiridates I was invited to Rome for a coronation, which was luxuriously organized.

*Tiridates III the Great
(painter M. Hovnatanyan)*

Coins from the Sasanid times

This way Tiridates founded the Arsacid dynasty in Armenia. During his reign Tiridates carried out a lot of wars, he is especially known for the expedition against the Alans (Ossetians), the tribe that penetrated the country from the north.

While the Arsacid continued reigning in Armenia, in Parthia the dynasty was defeated by one of Persian princes, Ardashir (Artashir) Sasanian in 226. The latter, gaining power, founded the Sasanid dynasty aspiring to get back the power of the Achaemenid era. Armenia became the main enemy of this new kingdom. In 252 Shapur I (Shapuh) conquered the major part of Armenia and appointed his son as the country's king. In the western part Khosrau II (Khosrov) Arsacid came to the throne with the support of Rome. Soon he was treacherously assassinated by the prince Anak (the father of Gregory the Illuminator). However, the Sasanid king declared war against Romans and left Armenians alone. The throne was occupied by Tiridates III, who played a role of uppermost importance in the Armenian history. It was thanks to him that Christianity was adopted in Armenia (301). In contrast to Rome, which allowed Christianity, along with other religions, in Armenia Christianity was recognized as the only official state religion in 301; the previous religion was persecuted starting from this period.

Khosrau III (Khosrov) substituted his father Tiridates, who aside from handling the politically complicated situation both within the country and outside (Roman–Persian relations, the betrayals of Armenian princes), also founded a new capital, Dvin, in the valley of Ararat. According to his order two forests were planted around the city. They exist till today and are named in his honor.

The fall of the Arsacid

Karmir blur cuneiform (VII century BC)

The following decades of the IV century were full of events. During the reign of the successors of Tiridates III, with constant fights between the Persians and the Romans, a tremendous interior confrontation emerged among the pro–Roman and pro–Persian nakharars (Armenian princes).

The interior disagreement and the betrayal of Armenian princes led to the division of the country between Rome (already Byzantine) and Persia in 387. Several western provinces went under the Byzantine domination, while the majority of Hayk Major territory became Persian. Until 428 the Arsacids were still reigning in the eastern part of the country. In 428, with the fall of the dynasty, Armenia completely lost its independence. However, it was during this ill–fated era for the Armenian nation that a new remedy was created, a new weapon to secure the existence of the people throughout the centuries: the Armenian alphabet was created by Mesrop Mashtots in 405.

The Sasanid Armenia

Being a part of the Sasanid Persia, the Eastern Armenia lost its independence, but preserved certain principles of autonomy. The political and economic position of the nakharars (princes) was quite solid. Very often the Armenian princes were appointed as governors. In the first period the Persian authorities showed tolerance towards the Armenian Church. Nevertheless, during the second half of the V century the situation altered. Persia increased the taxes and the highest posts were occupied by Persians.

The previous tolerance towards the Christian religion changed showing the tendency to force Armenians to accept Mazdaism, a branch of Zoroastrianism, which was threatening Armenian identity.

In spring 450 Persian authorities tried to force the Armenian population to accept the Persian religion. Uprisings took place having gained quite a massive character. Unfortunately, among the Armenian princes there was no unanimity.

The supporters of decisive actions got united around sparapet (the commander–in–chief of the armed forces) Vardan Mamikonyan.

On 26 May, 451 on the valley of Avarayr, to the southeast from the mountain Ararat, a battle of utmost importance took place. The words pronounced by Mamikonyan before the battle

"Vardanank"
(fragment, painter G. Khanjyan)

Emperor Justinian I (mosaic fragment of San-Vitale church in Ravenna)

converted into a slogan for the combatants of future generations "Conscious death is immortality, unconscious death is death". The battle was cruel for both sides. The sparapet himself died on the battlefield; there were no winners or losers. The Armenian resistance continued until the end of 451. Despite being lost, the resistance and the fight of the Armenians made the Persians give up certain positions. In 484, thanks to the new wave of rebellions headed by the nephew of Vardan Mamikonyan, a peace treaty was signed, according to which the auto–administration of Armenia was regained, which enabled Armenians to talk about a moral victory at the battle of Avarayr.

Byzantine Armenia

In the V century and in the first decades of the VI century the regime of nakharars did not considerably change; they themselves were leading the local army. The situation altered during the reign of the emperor Justinian I (527–565); he put an end of the Armenian autonomy, increased the contributions, and diminished the economic power of nakharars.

During the continuous wars between Byzantine and Persia, Western Armenia time and again became a battlefield. In the end of the VI century, due to the serious interior situation in Persia, the latter had to give the major part of Armenian territory to Byzantine in accordance with a new treaty of the year 591.

Armenia under the Arab Caliphate

■ *Model of the Catholicate in Dvin*

The VII century stands out for the change of the political situation in the Western Asia, caused by the Arab invasions. Creating a powerful state, the caliphate, which got strengthened by the religion Islam, the Arabs hit Persia several times during 630–640, conquered its western regions, invaded Mesopotamia, Syria, Palestine, Egypt.

In 640 the Arabs entered the Eastern Armenia for the first time, which back then belonged to Iran. After having destroyed the capital Dvin, they returned with a considerable amount of prisoners and plunder. In 642 the Arabs made the second attempt of conquering the country. The governor of Armenia Teodoros (Theodore) Rshtuni was able to resist them this time, as well as in 650, when he succeeded in returning back the plunder.

Nevertheless, taking into account the increasing power of the Arabs and the imminent danger they presented, in 652 Rshtuni himself recognized the power of the Arabs and signed a treaty with them, thanks to which, the Arab troops were withdrawn from Armenia. During the first decades of the Arab domination Armenia maintained relative independence.

In the beginning of the VIII century having finished the invasions and having already consolidated the power in the conquered territory, the Arab domination in Armenia acquired more cruel character; the taxes were increased and the religious intolerance augmented.

The chroniclers of the period describe harsh conditions of the population, unbearable taxes, prohibitions for constructing new churches etc.

The increasing pressure provoked protests of the people who rose against the Arabs during 703, 747–750 and 774–775.

The liberation fight was led by the nakharars (princes); among them the most prominent ones were the Mamikonyan and the Bagratuni (Bagratid). The latter were using more flexible policy thanks to which were enjoying the trust of the Arabs. The rivalry between these two families of nakharars converted into hostility. Finally, the battlefield was given up to the Bagratuni under the protection of which the independence of Armenia was recovered later in the IX century.

The most negative consequences of the Arab domination were the changes in the ethnographic structure of Armenia, a thing that had never occurred during the previous invasions. The Arabs set up their residence byrelocating native Armenian population. It was during the Arab domination that Armenians began leaving their historical motherland. Not being able to resist harsh social repressions Armenians fled to the neighboring Christian Byzantine

The Bagratid (Bagratuni)

■ *Coins of Barsegh*
(Basil) I

In 40–50 of the IX century the Arab power was decreasing, which was very beneficial both for the Armenian princes and the Byzantine Empire. Soon the Bagratid princes seized the situation. In 855 the Arabs withdrew their troops from Armenia and gave Ashot Bagratuni the right to collect the taxes and recognized him as a prince of princes. Nevertheless, it took a while for the Arabs to accept the situation. Consequently, they prepared a conspiracy against the Armenian prince, which failed due to Ashot's prudence, who fought against them in the outskirts of the city of Dvin. Getting convinced in the unanimous resistance of Armenians, in 885 the Caliph recognized Ashot Bagratuni as the king of Armenia. He was followed by the Byzantine Emperor Basil I, who originated from the Arsacid dynasty and who Ashot I had already set up an alliance with. (Note: Basil I is the founder of the Armenian dynasty of Byzantine emperors). The peace, however, did not last long; in 910 the Arabs, united with several Armenian princes, carried out a new attempt to overthrow the power of the Bagratid. The fight lasted until 921, when the king Ashot II the Iron defeated the Arabs on the shore of Lake Sevan.

Despite the fact that the reign of the Bagratid kingdom lasted short, it had an immense importance not only for the Armenian history, but also for the Armenian culture. Since 961 the capital of the Bagratid kingdom was the city of Ani, which was one of the most beautiful cities of the country and where famous architect Tiridates constructed his renowned cathedral. Because of the interior disagreements in the first half of XI century the power of the Armenian princes started giving in their positions. This was the chance that could not be missed by the neighbors: the Arabs and the Byzantines. The latter invited the Armenian king to Constantinople, where he was imprisoned. Despite the resistance of the inhabitants in 1045 they conquered Ani and put an end to the Armenian Bagratid dynasty. (The same dynasty continued reigning in Georgia).

The invasions of Seljuk Turks

After taking over Armenia, Byzantine reduced the Armenian troops to a minimum because of economic reasons. Therefore, the Seljuk Turks, who had already invaded Persia,

David IV Bagratuni

did not meet strong resistance, when crossing the Armenian border (1047, 1048, 1054). Byzantine did not immediately react to it, leaving Armenians alone to deal with the enemy.

The invasions of the nomadic tribes caused a great damage to Georgia as well. Nevertheless, by the time David IV the Constructor (1089–1125) got the throne, the decay of the Sultanate's power had already begun and the Georgian king started the liberation fight of Transcaucasian nations. The increasing power of Georgians was also motivational for Armenians. In the end of the XII century the decisive phase of the fight commenced, which was led by the sons of Sargis Zakharyan (he was the commander–in–chief of the Georgian army and Armenian troops at the court of David IV) Zakhare and Ivane, whose position gained a more solid stance after the throne was given to the queen Tamara (Tamar, 1184–1207).

After long years of a harsh fight the regions of Gugark, Artsakh (Nagorno Karabakh), Utik, Syunik, Ayrarat were liberated by Zakharyans (Zakarids), who, leading the rest of Armenian princes, established and extended their power until the invasions of the Mongols.

Cilicia

The world history knows no other example of a country's independence gained outside its territory. From ancient times Armenians lived in Cilicia (especially after the territory was conquered by the Armenian king Tigranes II). However, with the invasion of Seljuk Turks into Armenian territory, the number of Armenian population considerably increased, surpassing the number of the Greeks, Assyrians and Jews.

Major amount of people resettled in Cilicia after the fall of the city of Ani (1045). Among them were several Armenian princes, who used the unstable situation in the Byzantine Empire and tried to gain independence. In 1080 the prince Ruben succeeded in it. Counting on the support and assistance of the Armenian population, he displaced the Byzantines, founded the Rubinyan (Rubenid) dynasty that reigned since then in the Armenian principality of Cilicia. The fight against the Byzantine and afterwards against the crusaders, who were installed in the eastern part of the Mediterranean coast, was almost permanent. It was only in 1198 that the king Leon II (Levon) managed to found an Armenian kingdom in Cilicia.

The life of the kingdom had various periods. The most difficult phase started from the second

■ *Maritime fortress in Corycus*

■ *Coins of Levon II*

half of the XIII century with the invasions of mamluks, who were not always the winners, nevertheless, troublesome enemies for the Cilician state to face. After the continuous fights the capital of Cilicia, surrounded by enemies, had to surrender, having impoverished population, no food reserves and a wounded king Leon V of the recently established state. In 1375 the history of Armenian Cilicia terminated, having given the Armenian nation a three–century independence and a possibility to preserve its identity, culture and art.

Mongols in Armenia

Various tribes of Mongols (who were also called tartars) have lived in the territory between China and Siberia since the ancient times. In the beginning of the XIII century these nomadic tribes united and formed a country headed by Genghis Khan. (It can also be written as Genghis Kan, Gingiz Khan). During a very short period of time the Mongol hordes invaded an immense territory. In 1220 the Mongol army, composed of 20 thousand soldiers, entered Armenia and in 1236 conquered Armenia, Georgia and Albania (here meaning the Caucasian Albania). At the beginning of the XIV century it was already obvious that the Mongol state was decaying. The confrontation for the throne became more frequent. The khans were no longer able to lead such a huge country. During the second half of the same century the Mongol state collapsed; various principalities were established on its ruins. During the Mongol rule powerful Armenian principalities significantly weakened and started to collapse. Nevertheless, Armenia, devastated and exhausted because of endless wars, was destined to another challenge, a new misfortune – Tamerlane's invasions; his troops invaded Armenia four times starting from 1386. His reign lasted until his death (1405) and this period is considered to be the most macabre in the history of Armenia. After the death of Tamerlan Turkomen tribes (ak–koyunlu and kara–koyunlu) penetrated Armenia. While the nomadic tribes were taking over the country, the local population was emigrating unable to resist such harsh conditions. In 1410 the Turkmen already occupied the whole territory of Armenia. They reigned until the end of the century, gradually yielding power to the Armenian princes, while new threats, the Ottoman Empire from the West and Safavid Empire from the East, were rising for the whole region.

The division of Armenia between the Ottoman Turkey and the Safavid Persia

Due to its strategic importance Armenia was constantly disputed. On various occasions, the country was either under the domination of Persia or the Ottoman Turkey successively. It is worth mentioning that during the Turkish–Persian wars Yerevan changed its dependence 14 times during 1513 and 1737. Since 1514 wars started between the two increasing powers, threatening the whole population of the region. The Ottoman Turkey from the west and Safavid Iran from the east, whose territorial interests were not coinciding, were in constant wars for territory with a changing luck until 1555, when they divided Armenia between each other When in 1590 Shah Abbas occupied the throne, the situation altered. Having no desire to accept the defeat of his precursor, in 1603 he started a new war and re–conquered quite a lot of territory previously given to Turkey. One year later Turkey sent a big army against the Safavid Shah. The latter was following a very careful strategy; when there was a chance, he retreated, deciding not to risk his endeavor in the confrontation with a much more powerful enemy.As a part of this plan, the population was ordered to follow the Persian army during the withdrawal. Before abandoning the villages and cities, Persian soldiers were burning the fields and farms, as well as destroying the houses in order to leave the Turkish soldiers with no asylum and provisions and thus deprive them of the possibility to go farther. The tactics of devastating the land worked at a terrible cost for the Armenian population. It has been calculated that out of 300.000 deported people, only half survived the road towards Isfahan. Abbas established the khanate of Yerevan in the conquered territories.

Turkish–Persian confrontations lasted until 1639 when the Armenian territory got permanently divided. The part, which was under the Turkish domination, (more regions were given by the Soviets afterwards) nowadays forms Eastern Turkey. The Persian part, except for the contemporary territory of Armenia that was conquered by the Russian Empire later on, up to now continues to be the northern part of the Republic of Iran.

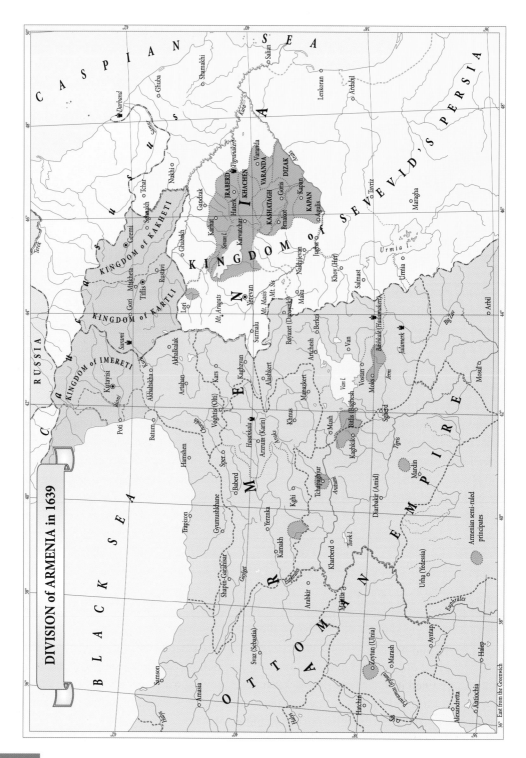

DIVISION of ARMENIA in 1639

C A S P I A N   S E A

B L A C K   S E A

KINGDOM of SEVEVID'S PERSIA

OTTOMAN EMPIRE

RUSSIA

KINGDOM of KAKHETI

KINGDOM of KARTLI

KINGDOM of IMERETI

KINGDOM of N.I.

Shamakhi
Salian
Lenkoran
Artabil
Shamakhi
Ghuba
Darband
Saliani
Tiflis
Tchar
Samakh
Nukhio
Gandzak
Kafan
Ghazakh
Sevan l.
Karvatchar
Tigranakert
Haterk
JRABERD
KHACHEN
VARANDA
Varanda
DIZAK
Goris
KASHATAGH
KAPAN
Brnakot
Agulis
Jughni
Nakhijevan
Maku
Khov (Her)
Salmast
Urmia l.
Urmia
Tavriz
Maragha
Arbil
Big Zav
Yerevan
Lori
Mt. Aragats
Mt. Masis
Mt. Sis
Surmalu
Bayazet (Daroynk)
Berkni
Artchesh
Van
Bashkale (Hadamakert)
Julamerk
Mosul
Mardin
Goris
Gardman
Mishketa
Gori
Rustavi
Gremi
Telavi
Erai

Poti
Kutayisi
Batum
Hamshen
Trapizon
Gyumushkhane
Shapin-Garahisar
Samson
Amasia
Siraz (Sebastia)
Kamakh
Kghi
Baberd
Sper
Yerznka
Arabkir
Kharberd
Tsovk l.
Zeytun (Ulnia)
Marash
Hatchini
Aleksandretta
Antiochia
Halep
Ayntap
Urha (Yedessia)
Dzumovmov (Ophon)
Malatia
Ardzun
Tchapaghjur
Mush
Bitlis
Baghesh
Kaghkiko
Sghert
Mosk
Vostan
Vantova
Van l.
Khnus
Manazkert
Alashkert
Kaghzvan
Aragts
E.
Voghtis (Olti)
Kars
Ardahan
Akhalkalak
Akhaltskha
Surami
Rioni
Tchoroh
Euphrates
Euphrates
Tigris
Tigris
Halis
Diarbakir (Amid)

Armenian semi-ruled principates

East from the Greenwich

36

The situation in Eastern Armenia (Persia)

Israel Ori

Being divided into two parts, the Armenian nation suffered very tough social and national repressions. During the second half of the XVII century and the whole XVIII century Armenians struggled to find ways of throwing off the yoke of foreign enslavers. The Armenian Church had an increasingly important role being the only institution that represented national interests in this struggle. Firstly, Armenians were looking for help among the European states. With this aim in mind the church was sending its missions to different European Governments, as well as Vatican. However, everything was in vain.

The increasing progress of Russia in the XVI–XVII centuries made Armenian socio–political classes regard it as an external power that is able to support Armenia in its liberation movement against Turkey and Iran. First and foremost, the fact that Russia's strategic and economic interests were to extend its territory towards Transcaucasia and gain access to the area of the Near East was taken into account. Here the interests of Armenia and Russia coincided. One of the most prominent figures of the Armenian liberation movement was Israel Ori, who played a significant role in the formation of the new political course of the Armenian nation.In the beginning of the XVIII century when all talks with Europe failed Ori went to Russia to start negotiations with Petr I. The latter promised to contribute to Armenian liberation movement.

Despite the difficulties of such a course, in the beginning of the XIX century Russia achieved certain success in Transcaucasia. Georgia and several northern regions of Armenia, Lori–Pambak and Shamshadin, became part of the Russian Empire in 1801. As a result of the Russian–Persian war of 1804–1813 Karabakh (Artsakh), together with other territories, also joined Russia. At the end of the 1826–1828 war the Russian troops succeeded in liberating Yerevan. Accepting its defeat, Iran had to sign a treaty of Turkmenchai in 1828, according to which, Iran recognized the Russian domination over Yerevan and Nakhijevan khanates. Furthermore, Armenians from Iran, as well as Western Armenia had a chance to move to the Russian part of the country. 40 thousand Armenians from Iran and 90 thousand Armenians from Turkey seized this opportunity. Thanks to this repatriation, the ethnic situation of the country changed and Armenians became the majority of the population once again.

Being the part of Tsarist Russia Armenian economy experienced a considerable rise. Agriculture remained its main branch. Nevertheless, starting from the second half of the XIX century certain changes happened in the industrial field as well: mining and food industries developed considerably. It is worth mentioning that Armenians were also working in Georgia and Azerbaijan (in Baku 53% of extracted petrol belonged to Armenian companies).

The situation in Western Armenia

In the second half of the XIX century the Ottoman Empire continued to be a backward state. The Turkish Government was trying to get out of feudal underdevelopment, make some bourgeois reforms. However, these superficial attempts did not involve all classes of the society and consequently did not deliver any result.

The overall situation in Turkey had its impact on the lives of the Armenian population. The life of a peasant was extremely hard, with an individual being subjected to cruel exploitation and national discrimination. Naturally, the existing situation was provoking protests among people over time acquiring the shape of uprisings and liberation fights. In 1860s in a number of Armenian populated regions people rose against the Turkish Government. The uprising of the Armenians of Zeytun is one the most notable among them..

They not only managed to prevent the attacks, but also to defeat the Turkish troops that were surpassing the Armenians in numbers. They managed it thanks to the mountainous relief of the region and the fact that Turkey did not want any interference by the European states that, in their turn, were aware of the situation and had their own interests. In the 1870s the fight of Balkan nations against the Turkish yoke strengthened further.

Well–known events, such as the Eastern conflict of 1875–1877, took place in the Balkans, grasping the attention of the European states that were eager to get the maximum out of the collapse of the Ottoman Empire. Russia was openly supporting the uprisings of the Slavic nations. During the Russian–Turkish war of 1877–1878 the Russian troops, among which there were many Armenian volunteers, liberated an extremely important part of the Western Armenian territory, including the cities of Kars, Erzrum, Bayazet and Ardahan. On the Balkan front the Russian troops overcame the Turkish resistance, entered Bulgaria, occupied Sofia and Adrianapolis creating a real threat to conquer Constantinople. This was a total defeat for Turkey.

On 3 March 1878 in San Stefano a peace treaty was signed stipulating the consolidation of Russia's positions in Transcaucasia and the Balkans: Bulgaria would acquire autonomy, Serbia, Chernogoria Montenegro and Romania would obtain independence.

Part of Besarabia, as well as the city of Kars and others, were transferred under the Russian domination. Another part of the Armenian territory, conquered during the war, was returned to Turkey. By the demands of the Western Armenians a new Article (n.16) was added to the treaty. It presupposed making reforms in the Armenian regions by the Turkish Government. Those reforms should have been guaranteed by the Russian troops that would be left in the territory of Western Armenia. Because of this article the question of the Western Armenians converted into a question of international relations: the Armenian Question.

The Armenian Question

Armenian delegation at Berlin Congress of 1878

The increasing power of Russia and the treaty of San Stefano was unsatisfactory both for Turks and great European powers, that had their own interests with regard to weak and deteriorated Turkey. England and Austro–Hungarian Empire demanded to hold a European congress. The congress took place in Berlin in the same year (1878) and as a result Russia had to cede a considerable part of its victory. Among others the Article 16 of San Stefano treaty got converted into the Article 61. The Article 61 of the treaty internationalized the Armenian Question to recognize the need of the reforms "of the regions inhabited by Armenians" by the Ottoman Government, as well as the responsibility of the European states to thoroughly supervise its fulfillment.

The following events demonstrated that Turkey did not comply with the requirements of the Article 61, instead carrying out its own project of "solving" the Armenian Question. After Berlin congress it was clear for Armenian people that they could only rely on themselves in solving this issue. Since then political and social organizations rose to fight for the freedom of Armenia. Troughtout the time these organizations these organizations turned into political parties, all with the same objective: the solution of the Armenian Question and the liberation of Western Armenians. However, it was evident that those organizations could not further expand their activities. For this reason they were being established outside Turkey, but even in Europe and Russia they were not able to act openly being constantly under surveillance.

Thanks to the opening of the Russian archives, it was subsequently proved that during the period of 1894–1896 Wilhelm II ordered his ambassadors in Russia, England and France to collect all possible information about Armenian nationalists in those countries and send it to Sultan. At the same time he ordered all the consuls in the Ottoman territory (who were working in various provinces) "to obtain information concerning Armenians living in their districts to transfer information to Abdul Hamid". More than 32 German and Austrian agents were gathering information about Armenians and sending it either to the German Embassy or Sultan directly.

These conditions forced Armenians to establish guerrilla organizations or fidayin (hayduk), as they called them. The main objective of the fidayin was to defend Armenian countrymen from persecutions and, at the same time, interrupt and impede the actions of the Ottoman Empire in the regions populated by Armenians. Anyway, their final mission was to regain

Khrimyan Hayrik (the Catholicos of All Armenians and the member of the Armenian delegation)

Armenian autonomy (being supported by the Armenian party Armenakan) or independence (parties such as Dashnak and Hnchak) depending on their ideology and the level of oppression of the Armenian population. This can be seen in the slogan of Dashnaks, which literally means "Liberty or Death".

Sabotage actions, such as cutting telegraph lines and attacking the warehouses with provisions of the army, as well as committing murders and counter–attacks on Muslim villages and assisting Armenian population in defending itself during the purges organized by the Ottoman officials were carried out. Fidayins were receiving full support of the Armenian population for this kind of actions and their fame began to augment rapidly. However, the Armenian liberation movement was isolated and did not have participants among other nations within Turkey. Furthermore, the Turkish Government was creating tensions between the Armenian and Kurdish people, utilizing the power of the latter in the fight against Armenians. Meanwhile, the Turkish Government was planning to settle the issues with the Armenian population putting an end to their liberation movement for once and for all.

Abdul Hamid II massacres

During 1894–1896 Turkish authorities organized massive slaughter of Armenians in Western Armenia and other regions of Turkey. In places like Sasun (1894), Zaytun (1895) and Van (1896) Armenian population firmly resisted. But the forces were not equal. In several provinces and cities the massacres were repeated. In total, around 300 thousand people died, hundreds of villages and towns were destroyed.

During those massacres both Western and Eastern Armenian social classes turned for help to European states asking to support Armenians in the Turkish Empire, urging for foreign intervention, that would cease the killings organized by Abdul Hamid. Their pleas remained unanswered.

The Young Turks

CUP (The Committee of Union and Progress) was the national reformist party of Turkey. It was formed as a secret student association. Its mission was to remove the Sultan and create laic state with civil rights and guarantees, including those for ethnic minorities.

Headed by Ismail Enver, Mehmed Talaat and Ahmed Jemal in 1908 the Young Turks came to the Subleme Porte and overthrew the Sultan. They wrote a new Carta Magna, established constitutional monarchy and appointing Murad V as a Sultan (Hamid's brother, who had been in prison for 33 years by Hamid's order). The platform of the Young Turks was promising equality for citizens, freedom of conscience, freedom of speech and press, parliamentary representation of the minorities and alike.

On 13 April 1909 a counter–revolution of the pro–Sultan forces broke out. The Young Turks received support of the Armenians and got back the power, oddly enough, on 24 of April of the same year. At the same time the massacres of Adana and Cilicia were organized causing the death of around 30.000 Armenians. Though it was reported that reactionist groups were responsible for these actions, it is well known that CUP was the one participating in it.

Progressive liberal ideas were cloaking the real aim of the organization: turkification of all social sectors of the Empire. Turkification is a synonym of Pan–Turkism (Imperial yearning to get united with Mongoloid race in Central Asia). There were only two obstacles on the way: Armenia and Russia.

WWI and the Armenian Genocide

The First World War broke out in August 1914: German Empire, Austria and Turkey against England, France and Russia (the states of Entente).

All Armenians, under the age of 45 living in Turkey, were obliged to enroll in the Ottoman army in order to fight together with Germany against the Tsarist threat. In the rival group, the Russian Armenians were the part of the tsarist army and had to serve on the European front. It was an appropriate time for the Turkish Government to execute their long–standing project of extermination and annihilation of the Armenian population within the Turkish Empire.

In April 1914 Special Organization (SO) was formed being comprised of ex–convicts, trained to get rid of Armenians on Turkish territory. On 15 April 1915 the leaders of Young Turks party Enver, Talaat and Nazim signed an order of deportation and extermination of the Armenian population. During the night of 24 April they started arresting Armenian intellectuals in Constantinople. They were arrested and deported to Anatolia; one part of them was assassinated on their way, the rest upon arrival. Distinguished Armenian poets such as Grigor Zohrap, Varujan, Siamanto, as well as numerous painters, writers, scientists and more than 4 thousand religious people fell victims to these massacres. Being unable to bear such a shock, a

■ *Exiled orphans*

Armenian girls, who became orphans as a result of the Genocide

prominent Armenian composer Komitas lost his mind.

Throughout a year massive deportation extended towards Mesopotamia and a desert, the area isolated from any conflict territory. Every Armenian had 2 days to abandon his house. The most influential and prepared Armenians were immediately executed. The rest of the population was forced to walk through the deserts towards the caravan, where indiscriminate slaughter indescribable abuse and torture towards women and children took place condemning those alive to slow death from hunger and thirst. There were more than 25 concentration camps in those exoduses, the majority of them open. The ships, loaded with victims, were sinking in the sea. The desert was covered with corpses with no graves to burry them in, until there was almost no one left. Out of 2 million Armenians less than 600 thousand survived the Genocide.

Those, who managed to escape the deportation, went into hiding with the support of their friendsacquaintances or missionaries, and fled wherever they could: Syria, Lebanon, Russia. From there they spread to all corners of the world.

After the defeat of Turkey in the First World War, the new authorities of the country convicted the Young Turks for being involved in the devastating war and handed them to justice. For some party leaders the sentence was carried out "from a distance", as many of them (Talaat, Shakir, Jemal, Jalil and others) had already fled the country. The Armenian national avengers carried out the sentences of some of them. In March 1921 an Armenian called Soghomon Tehliryan assassinated Talaat considering him being responsible for the massacres in his village. After fleeing the country, on 21 July1922 Ahmed Jemal (Cemal), together with his secretary were killed in Tiflis (Georgia) by the Armenian Stepan Dzaghikian, who was accusing him for being involved in the genocide of his nation.

The first Republic of Armenia

In February 1917, in the midst of the First World War, the second bourgeois–democratic revolution started in Russia. By that time economic and political situation of the Russian Empire was tarnished because of its participation in the war. As a consequence, the monarchy collapsed and Russian Provisional Government was formed. After February Revolution in Transcaucasia and other territories of the country a complicated process of power unification commenced.The main national parties were in favor of the new Provisional Government

*The coat of arms and
the flag of RA*

H. Qajaznuni

expecting the latter to make serious democratic reforms. Armenian national councils widened their activities in Tiflis (Tbilisi), Baku and Yerevan. In October 1917, taking advantage of the continuous crisis in the country and the protests of those who did not wish to continue the war, Bolsheviks easily removed the Provisional Government and seized the power. The government they created, the committee of popular commissioner headed by Lenin, approved a peace decree, which offered all combatant parties to cease the war and sign a treaty. In December 1917 the treaty was signed and the Russians started withdrawing their troops from Transcaucasia. The Bolshevik Government was ready to pay any price, even territorial, to get out of the war and sustain the power in its hands being hardly interested in the destiny of the Caucasus nations.

The national parties of Transcaucasia reacted with hostility to the news of the Bolshevik revolution. In order to impede the establishment of Bolshevik power in Tiflis, in November 1917 regional Governmental body, Transcaucasian Commissariat, was established (afterwards Transcaucasian Seim).

In January 1918 Turks violated the treaty and attacked the Caucasus front. Without encountering strong resistance, Turks conquered the region of Kars and Batumi. In April the representatives of the recently formed Transcaucasian Democratic Federative Republic held negotiations with Turkey. They resulted in the dissolution of the young republic (May 26) as the three parties, Armenia, Georgia and Baku, were not able to come to an agreement; Caucasian tartars were not going to impede the entrance of the Turks. At the time, when the Republic was splitting up, the Armenian troops were in battles in Sardarapat, Gharakilisa and Bash Aparan against Turks. On 28 May the Turkish forces were defeated, giving a chance to proclaim the independence of the first Republic of Armenia. In June 1918 Turkey recognized the independence of Armenia by Batumi treaty.

In July 1918 the new Government of the Republic was formed headed by Qajaznuni. The republic was established and operated under extremely hard conditions: being deteriorated by the war the country was at the edge of hunger. The Armenian Question remained the most relevant issue of the external politics. In the end of 1918 after the First World War and

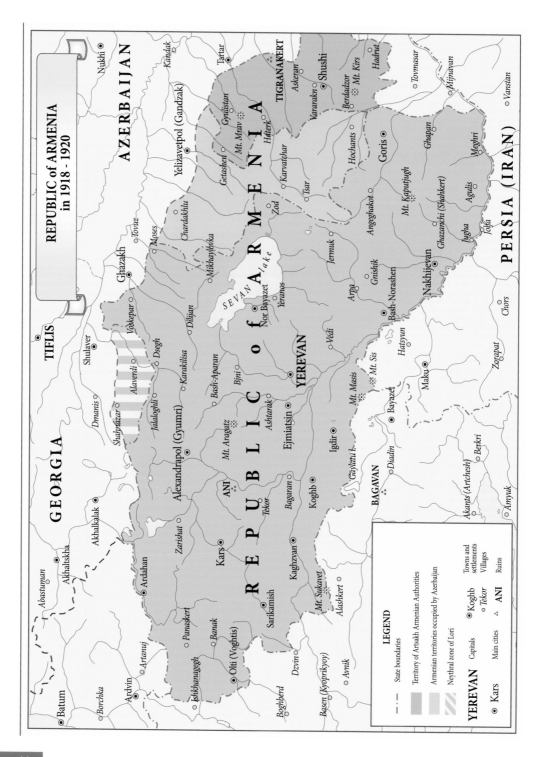

REPUBLIC of ARMENIA
in 1918 - 1920

LEGEND

State boundaries

Territory of Artsakh Armenian Authorities

Armenian territories occupied by Azerbaijan

Neytral zone of Lori

⦿ Koghb   Towns and settlements

○ Tekor   Villages

∴ ANI   Ruins

YEREVAN Capitals

⦿ Kars   Main cities

GEORGIA

AZERBAIJAN

TIFLIS

PERSIA (IRAN)

REPUBLIC of ARMENIA

TIGRANAKERT

BAGAVAN

SEVAN Lake

Batum
Borchka
Ardvin
Abastuman
Akhaltskha
Akhalkalak
Artanuj
Iskhkhanagegh
Basen (Kyoprikyoy)
Dzvin
Boghberd
Avnik
Amyuk
Dmanis
Shulaver
Zarishat
Panaskert
Banak
Sarikamish
Mt. Sukavet
Alashkert
Ardahan
Kars
Kaghzvan
Koghb
Bagaran
Tekor
ANI
Mt. Aragatz
Alexandrapol (Gyumri)
Shahnazar
Alaverdi
Talaloghli
Dsegh
Karaklisa
Bash-Aparan
Bjni
Ashtarak
Ejmiatsin
Igdir
Gaylatu I.
Diadin
Berkri
Akants (Artchesh)
Bayazet
Maku
Mt. Sis
Hatsyun
Mt. Masis
YEREVAN
Vedi
Nor Bayazet
Yeranos
Zod
Ternuk
Arpa
Grishik
Bash-Norashen
Zogapat
Chors
Nakhijevan
Ghazanchi (Shahker)
Mt. Kaputiugh
Angeghakot
Jugha
Jolfa
Agulis
Meghri
Ghapan
Goris
Hochants
Tsar
Karvatchar
Htaterk
Hdterk
Getashen
Mt. Mran
Gyulistan
Vararakn
Askeran
Berdadzor
Mt. Kirs
Shushi
Hadrut
Tovnasar
Mijnavan
Vanstan
Tartar
Yelizavetpol (Gandzak)
Kandak
Nukhi
Ghazakh
Toviz
Moses
Chardakhlu
Mikhaylovka
Dilijan
Voskepar
Olti (Voghtis)
Shalver

TIFLIS

Zogapat

44

RA Government building

at the beginning of 1919 Armenia succeeded in returning Kars, Alexandrapol, Sharur, as well as Nakhijevan. During the same period the people of Zangezur (Syunik) and Artsakh (Karabakh) were fighting against the Azeri–Turkish invaders, who wanted to take over the area. After lengthy negotiations the winner countries finally concluded the peace treaty in Sèvres in 1920. The articles of the treaty were highly favorable for Armenia. Turkey was to recognize the independence of Armenia; an access point to sea was to be returned to Armenia, which in total, would gain 160 thousand km². The nationalists, under the leadership of Mustafa Kemal Ataturk, spoke against the treaty, although the Sultan and the Ottoman Government accepted its terms. After taking the power Ataturk managed to maintain the possession of the whole Anatolia and part of the Eastern Thrace putting an end to the influence of France and Italy in the areas. Afterwards, the Treaty of Lausanne was signed in 1923 leaving the terms of the treaty of Sèvres unfulfilled. The relations between the first Republic and the Soviet Russia were not easy to maintain. The Bolsheviks had no interest in losing the Transcaucasian area. In September 1920 the troops of Kemalist Turkey entered Armenia. Being defeated by the enemy, Armenia had to recognize the power of the Bolsheviks who were helping to clear the country from the Turkish troops. Thus, on 2 December 1920 the first Republic collapsed and the Soviet Republic of Armenia was born.

The Soviet Armenia

The treaty signed between the Soviet Russia and the Republic of Armenia stipulated that Dashnakcutyun party would also have a chance to become a member of the Revolutionary Committee. However, this intension was never put in effect. The Bolshevik Government in Armenia carried the same changes as in Russia: the land, water, forests and subsoil, as well as industrial enterprises were nationalized putting an end to private property.

After joining the Soviet Union Armenia suffered immense territorial losses. Turkey and the new Socialist Republic negotiated the treaty of Kars, according to which, Turkey gave Adjaria to the USSR in return for acquiring the territories of Kars and Surmalu. The ceded territory included the ancient city of Ani and the mountain Ararat. In order to accomplish the will of Kemalist Turkey the Soviet Government attached Nakhijevan and afterwards Karabakh to Soviet Azerbaijan.

Starting from 12 March 1922 and until 5 December 1936 Armenia was the part of the Transcaucasian Socialist Federative Soviet Republic together with Georgia and Azerbaijan. Under the Soviet domination the Armenian population enjoyed a period of relative stability. On the other hand, it was very difficult for the Church to exist under the Soviet regime.

Stalin regime

In 1924 after the death of Vladimir Lenin, Joseph Stalin came to power. Stalin and his political cabinet drastically changed the economic and social structure of both Armenia and other Soviet states. In 1936 Transcaucasian Socialist Federative Soviet Republic got dissolved and Armenia, Azerbaijan and Georgia converted into separate Soviet countries. During the period of 25 years Armenia was industrialized and educated under strictly predesigned conditions where any sign of nationalism was instantly suppressed. Stalin took very severe measures to persecute the Armenian Apostolic Church (similar to Russian and Georgian Orthodox ones). In the 1920s the Church was deprived of its possessions. In the next decade the Soviets continued the discredit attacks against the Armenian Apostolic Church, which were terminated with the assassination of the patriarch Khoren I in 1938 as a part of the

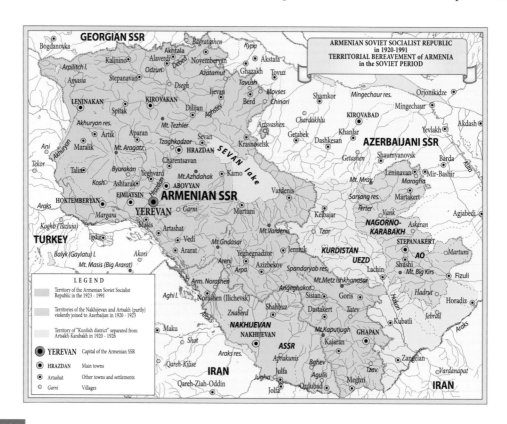

Great Purge. Fortunately the Church managed to survive in the Diaspora. Stalin executed and deported millions of innocent Armenians and other national minorities living in the USSR. In 1936 Joseph Stalin, together with Lavrenty Beria, worked on deporting Armenians to Siberia. Under his rule the Communist Party of Armenia used political terror to strengthen its political ideas among the population and suppress any expression of nationalism.Many writers, artists, scientists and political leaders were executed or exiled.

Armenia in the Great Patriotic War

H. Baghramyan

Armenia did not experience many of the devastation and destruction that shook the huge part of the Soviet Union during the World War II. The Nazis never entered the South Caucasus. However, Armenia played a valuable role in assisting the allies with its agriculture and industry. Moreover, the Armenians of the 89th "Tamanyan" Soviet Division were involved in brutal fighting against Wehrmacht in the Caucasus Battle, the Crimean Campaign, the Baltic Offensive, the Vistula–Oder Offensive and the Battle of Berlin. After the battle of the Hero City of Novorosiysk, which was taken by Germany, a lot of Armenians were included in the list of the Heroes of the Soviet Union. The Armenian General Hovhannes Baghramyan, later Marshal of the Soviet Union, was the first non-Slavic person to hold the position of front commander, when he was assigned to take the position at the First Baltic Front in 1943 with the mission to regain Dniester.

Nikita Khrushchev: the leader of the Soviet Union

N.Khrushchev in Yerevan

After the death of Joseph Stalin in 1953 Nikita Khrushchev emerged as the new leader of the country. Kremlin became permissive towards the demonstration of ethnic identities. The liberation wave started and was carried out from 1956 by Khrushchev (known as "the Thaw"), including partial rehabilitation. The process of denouncing Stalin's politics, promoted by Khrushchev, decreased the fear of many Soviet people. Moreover,

Lenin Square, Yerevan, 1961

he increased the amount of resources used for the production of consumer goods. Almost immediately Armenia began its rapid cultural and economic rebirth. Religion freedom was also regained and started openly operating after the Catholicos Vazgen I commenced his duties in 1955. On 24 April 1965 during the 50th anniversary of the Armenian Genocide thousands of Armenians initiated active demonstrations in the streets of Yerevan. The Soviet troops entered the city and tried to establish order. With the aim to prevent it to happen again, Kremlin permitted the construction of a memorial dedicated to the victims, who perished during those atrocities.

Leonid Brezhnev

On the one hand, the social life of this period was characterized by peace and stability guaranteed by the State; though still being a totalitarian country, it was not as brutal as during Stalin times; it became relatively benevolent. On the other hand, a lot of new cities, villages, factories, hospitals, universities and schools were constructed. The USSR was among a world leader in space exploration, aviation development, nuclear energy and fundamental sciences. However, incomes of the majority of the population were modest. The access to customer goods was also limited. The economy of the country was experiencing a period of so called stagnation, which was characterized by the deceleration of macroeconomic indicators (manipulated official figures), growing repressions towards the dissidents and the intellectuals, a renewed arms race against the United States, as well as the presence of the Soviet army in Afghanistan starting from 1979. Non–efficient local production, as well as increased corruption rates were highly affecting the economy of the country.

Perestroika

Huge changes took place in the USSR after Gorbachev took the office. The new political course called Perestroika (Reconstruction) received great support from the Soviet people who perceived it as the only way to get the country out of stagnation. Certain achievements were obtained quite fast: freedom of speech and democratization of social life. The politics of Mikhail Gorbachev enhanced the hope of the Armenian nation to live a better life under the Soviet rule. Armenians of the region called Nagorno Karabakh, which was annexed to Azerbaijan Soviet Socialist Republic by the Bolsheviks, started a peaceful and democratic movement to unite the region with Armenia. The majority of the people were tired of being forced to adapt to the culture of Azerbaijan. On 20 February 1988 the Armenian representatives of the National Council of Nagorno Karabakh voted for the unification with Armenia, which was immediately followed by ethnic disturbances causing a rupture between Armenian and Azeri population.

February demonstration 1988

Artsakh and Nagorno Karabakh conflict

Historically Armenian region of Nagorno Karabakh (native name Artsakh) was the last residence of the Armenian kings. Throughout years five small principalities were formed and existed in the territory until the arrival of the Russians to the Caucasus in the XIX century. As for 1920, when the Russian army occupied Azerbaijan and Armenia, Nagorno Karabakh and Nakhijevan were the part of the Republic of Armenia. Nevertheless, on 5 July 1921, based on the decision of Bolshevik party, Nagorno Karabakh and Nakhijevan were handed to the Soviet Azerbaijan with a majority of Armenian population, being separated from Armenia. In 1923 the autonomous region of Nagorno Karabakh was established. Previously the regions of Shahumyan and that of Getashen that had been part of Artsakh from ancient times, were separated from Karabakh. Azerbaijan's plan succeeded: the recently formed Azeri autonomy did not have any common frontiers with Armenia. Ever since a systematic Azeri persecution

Monte Melkonyan (legendary commander of the liberation fight of Artsakh)

of the Armenian population in Nagorno Karabakh was being organized with an intention to dispel them from the region and replace them with Azeris in order to take over the area both politically and ethnically.

During the Perestroika period the question rose again. In 1988 the first spontaneous demonstration took place in the Soviet Union; hundred thousand Armenian demonstrators demanded from Kremlin the reunion of Nagorno Karabakh with Armenia.

On 20 February 1988 the Regional Council of Karabakh (Parliament) during its XX special session decided to break the constitutional disposition of the USSR and turn to parties interested uniting Karabakh to Armenian Soviet Socialist Republic. The solidarity was extended all over the world, involving the whole Diaspora.

Armed groups of Azerbaijan carried out bloody pogroms of the Armenian citizens in the city of Sumgait (28 February 1988) and northern part of Baku causing massive death and displacement, forcing Armenians to flee. Those pogroms extended all over the territory of Azerbaijan, to the cities of Baku (black January of 1990), Kirovabad, Ganja and others.

The increasing inter-ethnic violence resulted in augmenting the number of casualties. This forced the Azeri population living in Armenia to get a refuge in their country and the Armenian population to flee from Azerbaijan. The control of the conflict seemed to be out of the Governments' hands; therefore Moscow's decision to take a direct control of the region in January 1989 was gladly received by many Armenians.

Armenian soldiers in liberated Shushi

President S. Sargsyan receives OSCE Minsk Group co–chairs (2010)

In summer 1989 the leaders and the followers of the Popular Front made Azerbaijan SSR start air and railway blockade against Armenia succeeding in strangling the economy of the country and impeding 85% of the cargo and goods imported to Armenia by the railway.

Another effect of this measure was the total separation of Nakhijevan from the Soviet Union.

In spring 1991 Gorbachev's Government held a special referendum throughout the whole country, called the Treaty of the Union, with the aim to decide whether the republics will continue being united. As a result, non–Communist Governments took over the offices in the republics with Boris Yeltsin in Russia, Levon Ter–Petrosyan in Armenia while Gorbachev was still in charge of the central Government as a president of the Union.

Azerbaijan voted for the fulfillment of the treaty, while some republics boycotted the referendum. Armenia held a parallel referendum on independence, which was declared on 21 September 1991 and where 99.8% of the population voted for it.

During this period many Armenians and Azeris of Nagorno Karabakh started acquiring weapons with an aim of self–defend. Moreover, Ayaz Mutallibov (the Head of the Council of Ministers of Azerbaijan) managed to get Gorbachev's support in carrying out a military operation together with the Soviet Army and the Azeri forces in order to disarm the Armenian militia.

This action was known as the "Operation Ring", which meant a forced deportation of Armenians living in the valleys of Shahumyan region. These actions were considered to be a method of intimidation both by the Soviet officials of Kremlin and the Armenian Government against those, who were raising the unifications demands.Armenian–American guerilla fighter Monte Melkonyan (who converted into one of the most efficient military leaders of the war) supported the idea that Karabakh must be liberated telling that if not done so, very soon Syunik would be annexed by Azerbaijan, which would be followed by the annex of the whole territory of Armenia, concluding that "the loss of Artsakh will mean the loss of Armenia".

Open war was declared during the dissolution of the USSR (1991). The Azeri militaries bombed Stepanakert, the capital of Artsakh, as well as other Armenian cities and villages bordering Karabakh.

The situation changed, when in May 1992 the Armenian army liberated Shushi (from where the bombarding of Stepanakert was carried out), which was of uppermost strategic importance and was occupied by the Azeri, and Lachin corridor, which is the only access to the region. As a result of these decisive victories the Armenian army liberated Nagorno Karabakh and partially Shahumyan and Getashen regions.

Since 1994 a ceasefire has been achieved in the region of Nagorno Karabakh thanks to the OSCE Minsk Group being comprised of Russia, USA and France, as well as Armenia and Azerbaijan. The truce has been grossly violated by the Azerbaijani side since August 2014. The situation reached an extraordinary escalation on the night of April 2, 2016.

Aggression lasted until the 5th of April, taking hundreds of young soldiers' lives.

The Armenian side once again fought back.

The government and the people of Nagorno Karabakh are committed to peaceful solution of the conflict supporting the idea that the only way to guarantee the security of the population is self–determination or a union with the Republic of Armenia.

Independent Republic of Artsakh

Capital:	Stepanakert
Population:	146 thousand inhabitants
Official language:	Armenian
Controlled territory:	12.5 thousand km²
Currency:	Dram

Coat of arms and flag of Nagorno Karabakh

Currently the Republic of Artsakh (Nagorno Karabakh) is a de facto independent state self–announced as an Independent Republic of Artsakh. It controls the major part of Nagorno Karabakh region and other districts of Azerbaijan, bordering Armenia in the West and Iran in the South. It is highly connected to the Republic of Armenia and even uses its currency, Dram. Armenia gives its citizenship to the inhabitants of Nagorno Karabakh. Nevertheless, Karabakh has its own independent government and economy thus preventing the repressions by Azerbaijan and those international communities who still consider Nagorno Karabakh to be an integral part of Azerbaijan. The politicians of Armenia and Nagorno Karabakh are so linked to each other, that the former president of Karabakh, Robert Kocharyan, was elected as the Prime Minister of Armenia in 1997 and President one year later.

Currently the negotiation process is in a deadlock, as both parties are unwilling to change their positions. Azerbaijan insists that the Armenian troops must abandon the region and the displaced population should return to their places of origin. In its turn, Armenia resists in

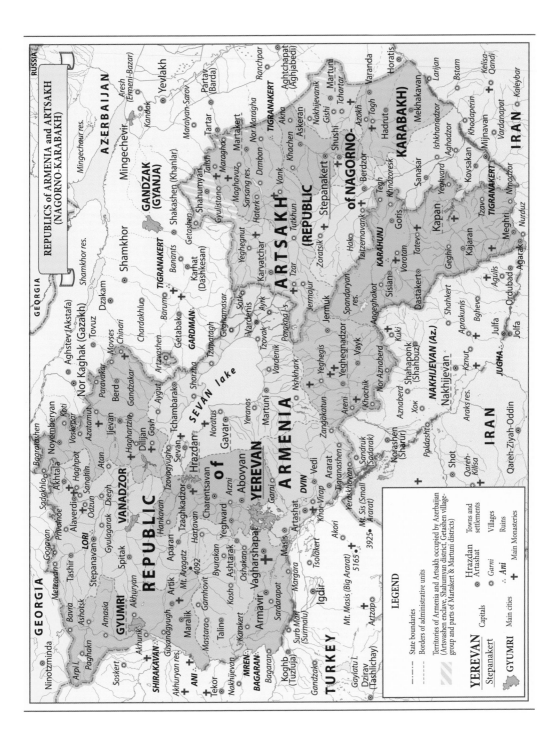

REPUBLICS of ARMENIA and ARTSAKH
(NAGORNO-KARABAKH)

LEGEND

-----	State boundaries
-----	Borders of administrative units

Territories of Armenia and Artsakh occupied by Azerbaijan (Artsvashen enclave, Shahumyan district, Getashen village-group and parts of Martakert & Martuni districts)

YEREVAN	Capitals
Stepanakert	
GYUMRI	Main cities

Hrazdan	Towns and settlements
Artashat	
Garni	Villages
∴ Ani	Ruins
+	Main Monasteries

accepting that Nagorno Karabakh is legally part of Azerbaijan arguing that Artsakh declared its independence simultaneously with Azerbaijan, so it is an independent country. Armenia also insists on allowing Nagorno Karabakh Government to take part in the negotiations.

Nagorno Karabakh is a presidential-parliamentary republic. The executive power primary pertains to the President. The President appoints and dismisses the Prime Minister. The National Assembly of Nagorno Karabakh is the legislative power and has 33 members; 22 are elected with a 5–year mandate individual constituencies and 11 by proportional representation. The Nagorno–Karabakh Republic has a multi–party system since 2009. The American NGO Freedom House ranks Nagorno–Karabakh Republic the at the same level with Armenia in terms of civil freedom and political rights.

The Ministry of Foreign Affairs is based in Stepanakert. The Nagorno–Karabakh Republic has five permanent Missions and an Office of Socio–Political Information in France.

Nagorno–Karabakh Republic is a member of the Community for Democracy and Rights of Nations, commonly known as the "Commonwealth of Unrecognized States".

NKR President's residence

Economy

Karabakh economy was highly affected by the war of 1991–1994. Currently thanks to the efforts of the local enterprises, as well as those from Armenia and Diaspora new factories, big and small companies are being established having a considerable influence on the development of the economy.

The existence of various kinds of wood such as ash–tree, beech and oak has enabled Nagorno Karabakh to set up wood industry. The factory of Drmbon, which extracts and processes gold and copper, is the most important enterprise of the heavy industry. Factories extracting various construction materials such as tufa, basalt, lime and granite also exist in the country. Mine enterprises are the main source of state budget. Energy industry is expected to bring high revenue. The largest source of electric energy is the hydroelectric power station on the river Tartar (Terter), with a capacity of 50 MVt. Food industry is also of high importance.

Nature

Artsakh is one of the most picturesque corners of the Armenian plateau. The major part of the territory is covered with mountains, the highest of which is Gyamish (3724m). The most important rivers are Tartar (Terter), Khachenaget that flow into the Kura, Khonashen and Ishkhan that flow into the Arax. The water from the rivers is used for irrigation, as well as for energy reasons.One third of the Republic is covered with forests that have large amounts of oak, beech and fruit trees. Among the widespread animals are wild goat, deer and wild boar.

The Republic of Armenia

Territory:	29 800 km²
Population:	2 979 900 (2017 Census)
Official language:	Armenian
Capital:	Yerevan
Currency:	Dram (AMD)

The modern Republic of Armenia is the third among the republics. The independence of the republic was proclaimed in August 1990. According to the results of the referendum held on the 21st of September 1991, 99.8% of the population voted for the independence of the country. The political system of the country was a presidential republic until the April 2018, and according to the RA Constitution the president was elected via the general elections for a term of 5 years, with the right to be reelected for a second term. A referendum to amend the Constitution was held in December 2015 and the country became a parliamentary republic. The critiques of the new constitution who considered the amendments as an effort

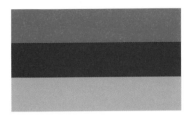

■ *RA coat of arms and flag*

of the governing president Serj Sargsyan to retain power after the termination of his second and last term of office stated the use of violence, pressure, fraud and falsification of votes for the amendments. Nevertheless, according to the results provided by the Electoral Committee of RA, the referendum was held with positive results and the constitutional amendments came into force in 2018. According to these amendments the president obtains limited representational responsibilities, the president appoints the prime minister of the country, however the candidature of the head of the Cabinet is suggested by the majority of the parliament, the parliament members themselves are elected to the National Assembly for the term of 5 years.

The Velvet Revolution

In the spring of 2018 the nomination of the candidature of the ex-president Serj Sargsyan for the office of the Prime Minister sparked a wave of mass peaceful protests and strikes in the whole country organized by the leader of oppositional parliament coalition "Elk" Nikol Pashinyan. As a result of the protests, Sargsyan and his Cabinet had to resign. The leader of the opposition Nikol Pashinyan was elected the Prime Minister. Extraordinary parliamentary elections were held in December 2018 where the coalition "My Step" lead by N. Pashinyan gained the majority of votes.

According to the head of the EU in Armenia, the events can be characterized as ideological revolution. The British journal "The Economist" named Armenia as the country of the year. The republic received this honor for the big step towards democracy. It should be noted that the change of power was done without bloodshed and victims.

Population

The population of Armenia reaches 2 million 998 thousand people (2016). The overall number of Armenians around the world is 12 million. Armenia is the only country of the former Soviet Union that has such homo–ethnic population: 97.7% are Armenians. The largest minority are Yazidis (1.3% – 40 600 people), Russians (0.5% – 14 660 people), Assyrians (0.1% – 3409 people), Ukrainians, Greek, Georgians and Iranians.

A huge wave of immigration of the 1990s, caused by the harsh economic situation of the country (economic blockade, paralyzed industry, unemployment, 1988 destructive earthquake and the war), considerably affected the demographic situation in Armenia. There are 48 cities and 915 villages in the territory of the Republic. The biggest city is the capital with a population of 1 million and 122 thousand people. The smallest town is Dastakert with only 300 inhabitants. The administrative division recognizes marz as the main unit (which is equal to a region). The country is divided into 10 marzes.

The official language of Armenia is Armenian (more precisely the Eastern Armenian; Diaspora speaks Western Armenian). Russian is also quite widespread and it is the second popular language. Except Armenian, the Yazidi minority representatives speak Kurdish. Other minorities use Armenian. The majority of believers are Apostolic Christians (94%). There is also a small community of Catholic Armenians, who are called "francos".The Muslim population, due to Nagorno Karabakh conflict, is comprised of small number of Iranians, who have a mosque in the center of Yerevan. There are also followers of Yazidism (more than 40 thousand people). The earthquake of 7 December 1988 with the epicenter in Shirak region destroyed the entire Northwest part of the country. The cities of Spitak and Gyumri were almost completely demolished. Stepanavan and Vanadzor were affected as well. More than 25 thousand people died. Another 20 thousand were seriously wounded. 500 thousand Armenians were left with no home and more than 170 enterprises ceased to function.

The reconstruction was implemented thanks to the external support including substantial

RA National Assembly

Independence Day of Armenia

aid from Diaspora. The reconstructed area consists of parts and districts built entirely with international assistance: Italian and Austrian districts, Norwegian hospital, British school and others. The Diaspora founded various support organizations for the Motherland including "SOS Armenie" and "Aznavour a Armenie". Though Armenia was then still the part of the USSR, the dissolution process, as well as the conflict with Azerbaijan had already begun and its imminence was more than obvious.

Economy

Armenia is an industrial–agrarian country. Its main natural resources are copper, lead, molybdenum, mineral water, precious metals and semi–precious stones. The economic activity of Armenia is mostly concentrated on 60% of the country given the complex geographic and terrain peculiarities. Armenia ranks 133 in the world by GDP (IMF list for 2018). The structure of GDP components for 2018: Industry (including energy sector) - 15.7%, construction - 7.1%, agriculture - 19.1%, service sector and trade - 50.3%. Approximately 75% of GDP is produced in the private sector. The major taxpayers of 2018 are Grand Tobacco, Zangezur Copper-Molybdenum Enterprise and Gazprom Armenia.

15 years ago the government of the Republic of Armenia announced that the IT sector was a prior direction in the country's economic development. According to the data provided by the Ministry of Transport, Communication and Information Technologies 15 000 jobs in the IT sector were established in 2017, 570 companies were opened. As the ministry informs there was another 10% rise in the number of workplaces in 2018. The share of the IT sector in the economy of the country is 4%. Armenia does not have proven oil reserves; it is imported from Russia and Iran. There are three gas–fired thermal power plants in Armenia (Hrazdan, Vanadzor and Yerevan) that produce 44% of country's electricity. Armenia also has hydroelectric power stations that produce 30% of the electricity. The largest hydroelectric stations are included in Sevan- Hrazdan (7 HPP) and the Vorotan (3 HPP) cascades.

During the Soviet times (in the 1970s) a nuclear power plant was constructed but was closed down after the horrible earthquake of 1988 (though the plant itself was not damaged). It started functioning again in 1995. Currently it produces 46-48% of the electricity. The nuclear fuel for the plant is extracted in Armenia. Thanks to foreign investments positive accomplishments were made in the industrial sector. In the last few years it became possible to partially resume the production in certain sectors that had been paralyzed because of the economic blockade, earthquake, Karabakh conflict and the collapse of the USSR.

Traditionally, the construction materials are tufa, basalt, perlite, marble, pumice, travertine, lime etc. Cement is also produced in Armenia. Based on the deposits of copper and lead in Kapan, Kajaran, Aragats and Akhtala, a copper smelter operates in Alaverdi. Aluminum, molybdenum and gold are produced from local raw materials. Diamond cutting is also carried out.

The chemical factory of Vanadzor is comprised of 25 enterprises. The chemical plant Nairit in Yerevan is functioning partially. There are various enterprises that produce pressing–molding machines, exact devices, synthetic rubber, plastic materials, tires, chemical fibers, mineral fertilizers, electromotor, software, microelectronics, jewelry, silk and alike. Wine-brandy production has actively grown in Armenia.

Agricultural work occupies 45% of the territory of the country with 20% dealing with cultivation and 25% with grazing. The biggest number of people is centered in the valley of Ararat, normally having harvest twice a year, as well as in the valley of the river Araks and the plains around Lake Sevan. The main agriculture products are cucurbitaceous, potatoes, wheat, grapevine, sugar beet, fruit trees, cotton, tobacco, tea etc. Stockbreeders are specialized in cattle; in the mountainous regions they breed sheep.

Foreign policy

The borders of the Republic of Armenia reach Iran in the South, Turkey in the West, Georgia in the North and Azerbaijan in the East.

As the borders of Armenia with Turkey and Azerbaijan are closed and the country does not have an access to sea, Georgia plays an essential role in the import and export of goods and productions. The countries are communicating via railway. Armenia exports electric energy to Georgia.

The relationship with Iran developed considerably after the collapse of the Soviet Union. In 2007 a gas pipe project was inaugurated;Iranian gas together with the Russian one is able to meet the needs of the country. In 2009 Iran–Armenia pipeline was put to use.

Despite not being an immediate neighbor, Russia has a lot of influence on Armenia. Russia is also one of the main investors in the Armenian economy (20 % of external trade). RA has been a member of the Eurasian Economic Community since 2013.

The Turkish–Armenian relations are complicated by Turkey's refusal to recognize the Armenian Genocide in the Ottoman Empire. Furthermore, during the Nagorno Karabakh conflict it blocked the Armenian–Turkish border. The existing trade relations with Turkey are non–official. On 6 September 2008 the President of Turkey Abdullah Gül paid a visit to Armenia. On 10 October 2009 in Zurich (Swtizerland) Armenian and Turkish ministers of Foreign Affairs Edward Nalbandyan and Ahmet Davutoğlu signed a protocol "On establishing diplomatic relations between Turkey and Armenia"

and a protocol "On the development of bilateral relations". The documents stipulate a creation of a commission comprised of "independent historians", who are called to examine the Armenian Genocide issue.

The following day the minister of Foreign Affairs of Azerbaijan sharply criticized Turkey for signing the treaties before the solution of Karabakh conflict. Consequently, Turkey did not ratify the treaty. The Republic of Armenia has participated in the European Neighborhood Policy since 2004 and in the Eastern Partnership since it was founded in 2009. In November 2017 a Comprehensive and broad partnership agreement was signed between Armenia and the EU in Brussels. The EU covers 22% of the Armenian Republic trade.

Armenian Diaspora

From the medieval times the Armenian nation was obliged to leave its land in a search of better and more bearable life conditions. This was caused by several reasons: the loss of independence, foreign invasions, ethnic and religious repressions. In the beginning people were immigrating to the nearest Christian countries (Byzantine, Georgia) afterwards extending their destinations to Bulgaria, in Crimea, Kiev Russia, Poland, India etc.

The fifth Pan–Armenian Games (Yerevan, 2011)

Modern Diaspora was formed during the years of 1915–1922 when the Ottoman Turkey committed the Armenian Genocide. Armenians that fled Turkey were scattered all over the world joining the Diaspora already existing in diverse countries. At the beginning it was very tough for the first generation of the refugees to start a new life; the majority lost their families and relatives and were left with nothing; among them were a lot of orphans, who in the majority of cases found asylum in Armenian orphanages. In general, the refugees received support and assistance of host countries and thus integrated rapidly into society. The next wave of immigrants left the country in the 1980–1990s because of the Nagorno Karabakh war, total unemployment and economic blockade (there was no electricity, water or gas in households).

The largest Armenian communities are;

Russian Federation:	1.8 million (Krasnodar krai, Stavropol krai, the Crimea, Rostov region, Moscow);
USA:	1.5 million (Los Angeles, Glendale, Fresno, Boston, Watertown, Detroit)
France:	700 thousand (Paris, Marseille, Lyon)
Georgia:	250 thousand (Tbilisi, Kutaisi, Kwemo Kartli, Abkhazia, Ajaria, Samtskhe-Javakheti)
Iran:	200 thousand (Tehran, Isfahan, Tabriz, Julfa, Urmia);

Syria:	130 thousand (Aleppo, Damascus, Kessab, Al-Qamishli). According to the recent news with regard to the current situation in Syria, more than 20 thousand Armenians were forced to leave their houses and 7 thousand out of them are currently residing in Armenia. However, the majority of these people do not lose their hope to return back home one day.
Lebanon:	120 thousand (Beirut, Anjar)
Argentina:	120 thousand (Buenos Aires)
Canada:	42 thousand (Montreal, Toronto, Quebec, Ottawa, Vancouver)
Ukraine:	150 thousand (Kiev, Lviv, Donetsk, Odessa, Kharkov,Luhansk)
Australia:	45 thousand (Sydney)
Brazil:	40 thousand (São Paulo)
Greece:	35 thousand (Athens, Thessaloniki, Pirey);
Uruguay:	15 thousand (Montevideo)

In Germany, UK and Spain the number of Armenian population varies from 15 to 20 thousand people in each country. All countries with Armenian communities have churches, schools, as well as diverse socio–cultural organizations. In some cities Armenians even have their own districts. It is worth mentioning that the political parties established before the arrival of Bolsheviks managed to continue their activities in the Diaspora. After the collapse of the Soviet Union the Diaspora, whose participation in the economic and political life of the Motherland was prohibited by the socialist system, acquired new opportunity to resume its relations with the Republic of Armenia. The Diaspora got especially active after the terrible earthquake in Spitak in 1988. The whole area was reconstructed thanks to the support and assistance of the Diaspora and international aid. French Diaspora created organizations like "Sos Armenie" and "Aznavour a Armenie" that still continue to implement support projects. National benefactor Poghos Nubar established another similar organization, Armenian General Benevolent Union, in 1906 in Cairo. This organization provides study grants for many Armenian students along with maintaining 30 Armenian schools. Patriotic unions support culture, art, Armenian language and poor families. "Hay Dat" ("The Armenian Tribunal") is dedicated to raising awareness of the Armenian among wider strata of the international society.

Armenia and the Silk Road

The Silk Road was a caravan route connecting Eastern Asia with the Mediterranean in ancient times and in the Middle Ages. First of all, it was used to export silk from China; this is where its name comes from. The road was made in the II century B.C. and had two main routes (the southern and the northern) and their branches. The term was put forward by the German geographer Ferdinand von Richthofen in 1877.

During the journey from east to west the silk was sold and bought dozens of times.

On the great trade road connecting Europe to Asia Armenia played a special role which was first of all was due to the country's convenient geographical position where the roads coming from Iran, the Central Asia, Mesopotamia and some distant regions crossed.

The trade route going through Armenia had a great influence on many layers of the country's cultural life. Armenia was first and foremost a transit country for the merchants from the East and the West, but the country itself took part in the trade with its own goods. Among them were expensive Armenian rugs, woolen fabrics, patterned scarves, shawls and leather goods. Textile products from Armenia were exported both to the East and West. Armenian cochineal, horses, jewelry, different oils and elixirs made from local herbs and plants were highly praised. From ancient times Armenia exported wine and grains to Mesopotamia. Armenia in its turn imported silk, precious and semi-precious stones, ceramics from China, Iran, from the countries of the Central Asia and Arab world, scented oils and elixirs. Armenian merchants had close commercial ties with such countries like distant India. According to Armenian historians in the 11th century the chandelier for the Cathedral of the capital city of Armenia was brought from India. At the same time Armenia was a transit country and due to it was getting rich. According to ancient authors, beginning from the II century Armenia was considered to be

Silk Road, Goris, XIX c.

one of the most important transit zones. According to international agreements the capital city of ancient Armenia, Artashat, was one of the most important trade-transit places for the caravans. Archeological artifacts found during the excavations also proved this fact. Mainly the excavations at the sites representing the Customs and the archive revealed thousands of seals from different parts of the world.

In the 5th century the new capital city of Armenia, Dvin, came to replace Artashat as a transit zone and up until the 13th century remained one of the major cities of the Middle East. The city as well as its goods was described by historians and travelers from different countries of the world with great admiration. According to the medieval Armenian historians the main international routes leading to China and India started from Dvin. The city had special storage area where silk was kept; this silk was later transferred to Byzantium. These storages were first mentioned in the 6th century.

A new route which connected China, Central Asia, Iran and Byzantium also passed through Dvin. This commercial route was also called the central route as it started from the central regions of China and passing through Loulan, Karashar or Karasahr and Kashgar reached the Fergana valley, then through Iranian Merve and other Iranian cities entered Armenia and through different routes reached Byzantium. Dvin-Trebizond route became the mostly-used road starting from the 10th

century. Trebizond was an important Black Sea port for Byzantium. Medieval sources as well as the ruins of Caravansarays indicate that caravans having left Dvin stopped in a small city called Aruch where in the middle ages Armenian troops used to be based and the city itself provided the capital city of Ani with agricultural goods. The city of Aruch had a big caravansaray which still stands in the same place half ruined. It is worth mentioning that in the 10th century exchangers in Aruch were exempted from taxes. After Aruch the route continued to the settlement called Talin where the caravansaray also had a big market, and then from Talin it went to Ani where at the entrance to the city there was another caravansaray.

Selim Caravansaray, XIV c.

By the way medieval caravansarays were of different types and under various terms. The caravansarays that are discussed in this book were close to the roads, were constructed every 30 km and were used for a short rest. In the cities next to the rest areas there were trade stalls and big storage zones.

Another route from Dvin lead to Iran and Central Asia and passed through Vayots-Dzor region. Eghegis settlement is worth mentioning as in the 13-14th centuries Jewish merchants lived there and one of the major arteries of the great Silk Road passed through the settlement, too. The presence of Jewish merchants there was quite interesting because the Armenian merchants were famous for being mediators between the West and the East. The Vardenyants Pass is situated not far from Eghegis: two caravansarays as well as the ruins of bridges constructed in different ages can be found up and down the Pass.

By the way, thanks to the Silk Road Marco Polo travelled through historical Armenia in the 13th century and left very interesting description of the Armenian cities and crafts.

King Abgar with the image of Christ (fresco, Varaga monastery)

The monument of Gregory the Illuminator in Rome (Vatican)

Christianity

According to historical records, Christianity in Armenia was preached by the disciples of Jesus Christ, apostles Thaddaeus and Bartholomew, who were martyred as the first Illuminators of Armenia. They are considered to be the founders of the Armenian Church. For this reason it is called Armenian Apostolic Church.

Before going further into the history of two apostles, it is worth telling the story of the Armenian king Abgar. According to Movses Khorenatsi (the Assyrian sources state the same), the king Abgar Artaxid, who lived in Edessa (Cilicia, currently Turkey) in the I century, sent a letter to Christ asking him to come to Edessa, to find a cure for an illness that was torturing him and stay permanently in Edessa free of Jewish persecution.

The Christ replied to him with Apostle Thomas' hands saying in the letter that he would not be able to come himself but promising to send one of his apostles to the king after his resurrection. The king's messengers, together with the letter, brought him the image of the Christ, printed on the handkerchief. After Jesus' resurrection the apostle Thaddaeus came to Edessa to cure the king. He also baptized him, his court and some citizens of Edessa.

According to Armenian sources after having cured the king in Cilicia, Thaddaeus left for Armenia, where Sanatruk (Sanatruces) Arsacid was reigning. The apostle travelled throughout the country, acquired many followers and baptized a lot of people; among them was the princess Sandukht. The king started persecuting the Christians. Even his own daughter was unable to avoid the persecution and shared the destiny of other martyred Christians.

6 days later by king's order the apostle Thaddaeus was killed in the province of Artaz (it was approximately in 66). The story of "Holy Lance" that was brought to Armenia is also attributed to St. Thaddaeus; currently this is one of the most important relics of the Armenian Church. A few years after the arrival of Thaddaeus to Armenia the apostle Bartholomew

Apostles Thaddaeus and Bartholomew

repeated his path along with eight Persian followers. He found an asylum in the province of Goghtn, where he was kindly received by the local prince. Bartholomew was preaching among various social classes, including the court. He succeeded in converting king Sanatruk's sister and several commanders into Christianity. Based on the king's order all these people were martyred.

The same destiny was prepared for the apostle himself, who died in Aghbak approximately in 68. Nevertheless, it did not take too much time for the seeds sown by the apostles to grow. The history of the adoption of Christianity reached us thanks to the chronicler Agatangeghos, whose history is completed with that of other historians.

Gregory the Illuminator was the son of the prince Anak Arsacid, who came to Armenia obeying the order of the Persian king Artashir to assassinate the king Khosrau (Khosrov). After having spent two years in the Armenian court Anak completed his horrible plan. When he tried to escape to Persia, he got detained and assassinated by Armenian princes together with his family.

Only one of Anak's sons, Gregory, survived. A person called Evtagh, who saved the child, took him to Caesarea (Cesaria), where Gregory acquired Christian knowledge. In 287, when the son of the assassinated Khosrau, Tiridates, being supported by Roman troops, came to Armenia to get the throne, Gregory joined the troops of the Armenian king and fought with him against Persians.

King Tiridates was celebrating Persians' defeat in Eriza village in the province of Ekeghyats in one of the temples of the Goddess Anahit (the main Goddess in the Armenian mythology) offering her many sacrifices. Among others Gregory also had to demonstrate his gratitude towards the pagan Goddess offering her a sacrifice of flowers. Gregory refused to do it, thus revealing to everyone that he was Christian.

For refusing to obey the king's order Gregory was sentenced to torture.

Even after these inhumane tortures Gregory stood firm in his belief. The wrath of the king was limitless, when he discovered that Gregory was the son of his father's murderer. Gregory was imprisoned in one of the dungeons near Artashat. He spent 13 years here (or 13 months, weeks; the translation from the archaic Armenian presents some doubts on that matter), but managed to survive thanks to a woman, who was daily bringing him food. The adoption of Christianity in Armenia is closely tied to the tortures and deaths of the saint Hripsime and other nuns.

The tradition tells that being saved from emperor Diocletian's intolerant attitude towards the Christians, a group of nuns, led by Gayane, left for Armenia. Among them was beautiful Hripsime. Diocletian sent a letter to the Armenian king exhorting him to find the nuns and send them back to Rome.

The nuns were found in the valley of Ararat and brought to the palace. Fascinated by Hripsime's beauty the king offered her to marry him but was rejected by that nun. All 37 nuns were martyred in the year 301.

The story of the nuns of Hripsime has a decisive role for the history of Armenia. After killing Hripsime, Tiridates fell into a grave psychiatric state, suffering from a disease called lycanthropy (a type of Schizophrenia, when a person loses his mind and imagines himself an animal.Similar disease was also mentioned by prophet Daniel affecting the Babylonian king Nebuchadnezzar) and imagined that he was a wild boar.

No remedy could cure the disease. The sister of the king, Khosrovdukht, told his brother to pray to the Christian God because his disease was a punishment for having tortured the nuns. Khosrovdukht's persistence resulted in the king's decision to free Gregory from the dungeon. To everyone's surprise he was still alive. Gregory cured the king with his prayers.He preached Christianity among the court and common folk for 60 days.

On the last day he had a vision of the Christ coming down to the Earth (the tradition says that he was holding a golden hammer) and showing the place where a church should be built (Ejmiadzin).

In 301 Armenia officially converted into a Christian country. The fact that even without having missioners at his disposal it did not take Gregory much time to Christianize the whole country proves that Christianity already existed in Armenia.

Dogmas of the Armenian Apostolic Church

The Armenian Church recognizes the first three Universal Councils. After the Council of Chalcedon (the Council is considered to be the Fourth of the first six Ecumenical Council of Christianity) in 451 the Armenian Apostolic Church, together with the Patriarchate of Alexandria and Jacobite Church, broke the previous agreement of the Council of Ephesus (425) and produced a relapse in Nestorianism.

Thus, formally they broke the communion with the Pope and the rest of the patriarchs being referred to as split monophysites. However, The Armenian Church does not consider itself to be a monophysite(this opinion is erroneous). The Armenian Church rejects two extremes: both the dogmas of the followers of Arius, who only recognize the human nature of Jesus Christ, and the dogmas of the followers of Eutyches, that only accept the divine nature of Jesus Christ.

The Armenian Church accepts the following doctrine: "a divine being, two perfect natures of divinity and humanity harmoniously united in one, one united will, sole harmonic unified energy. As the incarnation of the Christ is the incarnation of the God–Man, in the incarnated Christ there should be one sole will of the God–Man being comprised of two. If we deny the existence of one harmonious will, this will mean that no complete, entire, harmonic incarnation took place.

The dogmatic base of the Armenian Church is the Symbol of Faith,precisely from the harmony of nature, energy and will in the Incarnation of the Christ. The symbol contains the formula of Saint Athanasius created during the Council of Nicaea in the IV century.This formula exceptionally well catches the doctrine of Incarnation preserved without changes and additions.

Being motivated by this fact both idolatry and images of saints in the houses were prohibited by the Armenian Church.

As for the paintings and bas-reliefs that are present in Armenian churches and cathedrals it should be mentioned that they are consecrated with myrrh thus differing from the ordinary art works.

The Armenian Church prefers simplicity and avoids exaggerations in its doctrines. The principle of "the freedom to doubt" is fully applied by the Armenian Church.It is believed that only when following this principle it is possible to talk about "compassion towards everyone".

Sacraments

Catholicos Vazgen I

The Armenian church, like the Roman Catholic and Orthodox Churches, accepts seven sacraments: Baptism, Confirmation, Holy Communion, Confession, Holy Matrimony, Holy Orders, Anointing of the Sick or Extreme Unction. But with regards to the administration of the sacraments, it has its own ways.

The Armenian Church performs the ceremony of Baptism merging the baby into the water three times in remembrance of three days of Jesus' burial, though sprinkling is also permitted.

The Confirmation and the first Communion are performed together with Baptism; only with the fulfillment of all three sacraments Baptism can be considered real.

During the Confirmation the Holy Myrrh is anointed on nine parts of person's body; forehead, eyes, ears, nose, mouth, heart, back and knees. The Armenian Church also performs the

Palm Sunday

Confirmation, which confers the baptized persons the mercy of the Holy Spirit. The material symbol of the Holy Spirit is the Holy Myrrh (Holy Oil) made of a variety of flowers and perfumed oils. The Holy Myrrh is prepared and blessed every seven years by the Catholicos of all Armenians with always adding whatever is left of the previous one into the Myrrh. Afterwards, it is distributed to other Armenian churches all over the world. The Holy Oil is the symbol of unity of all the Armenians in all times. The Holy Communion is performed during the Baptism and after the High Mass. Any believer despite gender and age can take the communion. According to the custom the believer must take Holy Communion at least during five big holidays: Christmas, Easter, Transfiguration, Assumption of Mary, Feast of the Cross. The hostia (sacramental bread) is always unique. The sacrament is administered in small pieces soaked in pure wine. Armenian Church has two types of confession of sin; individual and collective. It should be mentioned that the Armenian Church has never had confessionals (confessional booths). Holy Ordination is received by the clergy (priest, bishop). The Matrimony can be performed by a priest. Visitation of the Sick. The Armenian Church prays for the sick but does not anoint them because at the moment of the confirmation a child has already been anointed. The sacrifice of the animals (matagh), despite not being a sacrament, is a custom that dates back to the ancient times. The animal sacrifice is performed to thank the God for his beneficence. The meat should be divided into seven (or three) portions and distributed among the poor. The participation of the priest in the sacrifice is limited; he does nothing but blessing the salt with which the meat is seasoned.

Hierarchy in the Armenian Church

The administrative and pastoral head of the Armenian Church is the Supreme Patriarch or the Catholicos of All Armenians.

During the period of Gregory the Illuminator the residence in Ejmiadzin was constructed only 21km away from Yerevan.

In its turn, after the collapse of the kingdom of Cilicia the Catholicos took religious and political matters of the nation into his own hands, since there was no other king except the Sultan of the Ottoman Empire.

The internal organization is one of the peculiarities of the Armenian Apostolic Church. After the relocation of its residence during the Middle Ages rivalry between four divided jurisdictional centers began: Armenian Patriarchate of Jerusalem, Armenian Patriarch of Constantinople, Holy See of Cilicia and the Supreme Patriarchate of the Catholicos of All Armenians. Until the massacres of the beginning of the XX century another patriarchal center existed also in Akhtamar (Lake Van, currently in Turkey). The majority of those faithful to the Armenian Church recognize the Catholicos as a spiritual leader.

Ejmiatsin Cathedral

*Fragment of a dome,
Ejmiatsin Cathedral*

Currently two jurisdictional centers (Jerusalem and Constantinople) also recognize the Catholicos as the head of the Armenian Church and are in full communion with him.

The Catholicate of Ejmiadzin has jurisdiction over all Armenians living in the territory of the former Soviet Union and almost all Armenians in Diaspora.

Nowadays there are many large Armenian apostolic congregations in many countries outside Armenia including Russia, Iraq, Georgia, France, US, Lebanon, Syria, Canada, Australia, Cyprus, Israel, Greece, Bulgaria, Belgium, Egypt, Estonia, UK, Germany, Italy, the Netherlands, Switzerland, Sweden, Argentina, Uruguay and others.

The Armenian clergy hierarchy has the following form: Catholicos, bishop, archimandrite, priest, deacon and clergy; the latter has his subtitles: lamplighter, sacristan, exorcist, key holder. Before the consecration a priest has to either get married or take a vow of celibacy. A single priest wears a conical cap as a symbol of his resignation. Married priests are not deprived of the right to fulfill the sacraments.

The Catholicos is appointed by the Synod; the elections are comprised of two phases. During the first one five bishops are elected. During the second round Catholicos is chosen out of the five elected candidates. Catholicos is elected for life. After the elections 12 bishops anoint the Catholicos with the holy Myrrh.

The current Catholicos of All Armenians is Garegin II occupying the position since 1999.

Architecture

The Armenian architecture has its distinctive style typical for different periods of Armenian history.

In I millennium BC the formation of the Armenian nation was coming to an end. During this period the Armenian tribes that were the majority of the population in Urartu kingdom were dedicated to the construction of fortresses, citadels, water pipes. The examples of this can be found both within the country, as well as in modern Turkish territory (city of Van in Turkey, Erebuni fortress in Yerevan, Argishtikhinili).

The entrance of Erebuni fortress 782 BC

Starting from the VI century BC the Armenian architecture and urbanism entered a new period. The first mentioning of the popular Armenian house "glkhatun" can be found in Xenophon's "Anabasis". During III–I centuries the cities of Armavir, Yervandashat, Artashat, Tigranakert and others emerged and developed during the Armenian state. Metallurgy, pottery, artistic treatment of stone and wood, construction were developed in big cities. Starting from the

Dome, Haghpat Monastery

Ani Cathedral

IV century BC the architecture of these cities, as well as that of big fortresses and pagan temples started developing under the influence of Greek–Hellenistic and Roman cultures, establishing the "Armenian Hellenism" starting from the I century. According to Plutarch there were theaters styled as ancient amphitheaters, bathhouses with mosaics, water supply systems etc in Artashat and Tigranakert.

It is only after the adoption of Christianity that one can talk about Armenian religious architecture. Mostly, the churches from the IV–V centuries are basilicas (Kasakh - IV c., Akhts - IV c., Eghvard - V c., Tekor - V c., Yereruyk - V c., Dvin - V c.). Yereruyk church that has some similarities with Syrian Christian architecture of early middle ages stands out among them.

From the V century basilicas were substituted with domed churches with various architectural representations. This inspired the development of domed halls (Ptghni VI–VII century, Aruch (639-661), domed basilicas (Odzun VI century, Mren 613–640), as well as domed basilicas with a triple–apse (Talin cathedral VII century, St. Gregory of Dvin 608–615).

The cruciform temples with centered domes from VI–VII centuries are more varied. During this era the Armenian architecture was leaning towards the integrity of interior space. This architectural idea was developed in the church of Avan (588–597) and reached its classic perfection in the church of St. Hripsime (618) and others (Artsvaberd VII century, Targmanchats VII century, Aramus VII century, Sisavan VII century). Here the ideas of interconnection of the architectural plan, shapes and perspectives, integrity of architectural idea are performed with maximum accuracy and laconism. Mastara (V–VI centuries), Artik (VII century), Voskepar (VI–VII centuries) represent the type of four–apse, center domed cruciform churches.

The aspirations to create new type of cruciform center domed churches led to the construction of the masterpiece of the Armenian architecture, Zvartnots temple (641–652), which is also distinguished by its decorative principle of architectural construction.

At the same time during the V–VI centuries the styles of small churches with a cruciform floor (ground plan) (Karmravor VII century, St. Sergey Bjni VII century) and domical basilicas with octagonal tambour (St. Stephan of Lmbatavank VI century) were elaborated.

The architecture of laic buildings was developed independently. The palaces of Dvin (V and VII centuries) and Zvartnots (VII century) and the palace of Aruch stand out for the unity of the compositional solution of the structure. The chapterhouses occupy the central role there.

It is typical for the churches of this period to have rectangular structure, where the cross is installed being formed with four apses; the majority is of semi–circular shape with two

axes of symmetry. From the first construction up to now the main apse is directed to the East. The lateral altars are square; the interior is rich with spatial forms. The culmination of shapes is the dome. The harmony of the interior volumes with those of the exterior is highlighted by façades, which are decorated with niches the chiaroscuro of which brightens up the façade and emphasizes its composition.

In the V–VII centuries the roof was made of baked clay tiles and from the IX century of stone tiles. The solidity of the buildings and their resistance to earthquakes was the main issue to worry the architects. The stone brickwork of two parallel rows and the strategy to fill in the space between them with adobe fostered the development of vaulted, bent and domed buildings. This system of brickwork called "midis", attested throughout centuries, is still used nowadays.

According to specialists the appearance of the first monastic complexes dates back to the VII century and reached its florescence in the XII century. There are usually comprised of series of elements: the main church, other churches, atrium (gavit), chapel, sometimes a bell tower, refectory, library, cells (prison) and administrative constructions. Very often the complex was surrounded by walls, where the economic and residential constructions were situated.

The complex was not built immediately; other buildings were gradually attached to the main church. The task of the medieval architecture consisted of attributing certain equilibrium to this group of complicated constructions. The atrium, being an integral part of the complex, is attached to the church and normally has a shape of a hall with four or no columns, which sustain the dome along with cross arcs or extended arcs among columns and walls; the dome has a circular hole in the center (also called chimney or beacon).

Together with the construction of medieval monasteries and fortresses the construction of bridges, caravanserais, mills, irrigation system, roads etc. was also progressing.

The concept of residential houses elaborated in the Middle Ages has not changed throughout centuries. According to N. Marr the houses of the citizens of Ani in the XII–III centuries were made of stone and had two floors. The first floor served for economic reasons (wine cellar, warehouse). The vertical oven "thonir" was also located on the first floor. The rooms were on the second floor situated in one or two rows. During XVIII–XIX centuries houses preserved their two–floor structure but differed due to small balconies or rich wood decoration along the whole façade, a very typical element.

Khachkar

Khachars occupy a special place in the Armenian architecture. Khachkar, which is a stele with carved cross in the center, is translated into English as "khach"– cross and "kar"– stone. The theme of rectangular stelas dates back to pagan times. Since the second millennium in the territory of the Armenian plateau vishapakars (dragon stones) were being installed. After adopting Christianity, steles changed the themes; images of Tiridates III and Gregory the Illuminator were carved on them. People used to make the cross stones and take them to churches. During V–VI centuries the stones made of wood were substituted by cross stones. In the VII century crosses with "arms" (sculpted crosses) appeared. Later they acquired a shape of a cross, carved on the rectangular piece of stone. The most ancient of the preserved khachkars dates back to the IX–X centuries.

The art of carving stone has reached such a level that it can be correctly compared with the work of refined jewelry or delicate filigree. Rightly enough, some khachkars are also called "embroidered".

In the center of a khachkar there is an Armenian flowered cross; being the symbol of Jesus it represents life and salvation. Around the cross there are rosettes, flowers, eight point stars, birds, fruits, animals, various ornaments and motives. It is an expression of the genius, mastery, that of the eagerness, desire and imagination of the "varpet" (master in Armenian). The prominent Greek scientist Mitsos Alexandroupoli expressed his great surprise when describing Armenian khachkars: "They convert the stone into an embroidery, carpet, garden or song". In November 2010 the art of carving khachkars was included in the UNESCO Intangible Cultural Heritage List.

Khachkar, Noravank, XIV century

Vishapakar (Dragon-stone), Geghama mountain chain, II mil. B.C.

Climate Relief Nature Subsoil

The Republic of Armenia is situated in the Northeast of Armenian high plateau. 50% of the territory is at 2000m above sea level. The average height is 1700–1800m. The highest point is the mountain Aragats at 4090m. The lowest point is the area of the low flow of the Debed river, 375m. In the North and East Armenia is surrounded by the Caucasus Minor mountain range. In the central part of the country there are solid volcanic masses and in the Southwest the valley of Ararat is located. In the southern part of the country stretches Zangezur mountain range, which is the highest in the plateau of the Caucasus Minor. The territory of Armenia belongs to the area of young alpine fault–bend fold, which conditions the formation of mountains with occasional destructive earthquakes as a consequence. The earthquakes of Leninakan (1926), Zangezur (1931), Yerevan (1937) and the devastating one in Spitak (1988) serve to illustrate this point. The maximum magnitude of earthquakes in Armenia is 10 points by the scale of 12.

The climate of Armenia is conditioned by particularities of subtropical zone and the relief. During the year there are no regular precipitations; those happen mainly in spring and in the beginning of summer, 600–700mm a year. It snows often during winter in Armenia; by average calculations 100cm a year. Similar to other countries with same terrain, temperature falls down while climbing the mountain; one degree every 200m with the amount of precipitations increasing. The average temperature in Ararat valley in July is +25°C +27°C and the absolute maximum is +42°C. In January the average temperature is –5°C –7°C the absolute record being –30°C. In central region (the area of Lake Sevan) the average temperature in summer is normally +18°C +20°C and the absolute maximum temperature is +35°C. In winter the average temperature can be –8°C –12°C;the absolute minimum is –38°C. The absolute minimum temperature of –46°C was registered in the area of Lake Arpi. The average number of frost–free days in Armenia is 250 in Ararat Valley, and 150–200 days in central areas.

The maximum of 30–50 days are considered frost–free in upper elevations. It is typical for Armenia to receive an average of 2700 hours of sunlight a year.

There are 565 deposits of 60 useful minerals in the Republic of Armenia. The resources of gold constitute 0.4%, silver 0.5. %, zinc 0.3%, copper 0.9%, molybdenum 7.6% of the world resources. Armenia is also rich with natural stones: tufa, granite, basalt etc. Construction stone reserves estimate is around 960 million m³. It also possesses a big variety of precious and semi–precious stones. Armenia is rich in natural minerals; the resources of perlite reach 160 million tons and, according to preliminary calculations, the resources of rock salt can reach up to ten thousand million tons.

There are around 7500 springs of drinking water in Armenia. 1300 of those are of mineral water; part of them is of special significance in terms of health. 9480 big and small rivers run through the territory of the country and 379 of them have more than 10km in length. 75 water deposits have been constructed on the rivers. There are 100 small lakes with around 300 million m³ water including the largest mountainous Lake Sevan. The country is rich with underground water having 3 million m³ of water a year. In Ararat valley, because of the tension of artesian water due to the irregular distribution of underground streams, swamps are often formed with a surface of 1500 m².

In Armenia there are approximately 3200 species of plants, which is the result of Armenia being situated between two geo–botanic zones: the Caucasian forest–meadows and the desert/semi–desert of Iran. The forests, which comprise 12% of the territory, extend normally in the mountains. The widespread trees are oak, beech, carp, linden, maple, ash pine and a great variety of wild fruit ones. It is typical for plain areas to have steppe vegetation. In rocky and stony areas there are many bushes: almond, buckthorn, astragalus, as well as thyme, clary

Waterfall in Jermuk

sage etc. From the floristic point of view Armenia is the country of interesting discoveries.

The fauna of Armenia includes more than 10 thousand species of invertebrates, almost 450 species of vertebrates; among them 76 mammals, 304 species of birds (100 overwintering), 44 species of reptiles, 6 species of amphibians and 24 species of fish: common barbel, varicorhinus capoeta (khramulya of Sevan), Sevan trout, swindler. Numerous rodents inhabit the steppe and semi–deserts such as mole rats, jumping mice as well as gopher, Greek turtle, small lizard, and Armenian viper from the reptiles.

In Arax valley one may find wild boar, jungle cat, jackal; from birds; duck, goose, lark, hoopoe, crane, stork, partridge, quail, capercaillie, eagle, seagull (in Lake Sevan area). In the mountains there are lynx, bear, roe deer, mouflon, wild goat and very rarely leopard.

Stalactite Caves, Vayots Dzor

The Symphony of Stones,
Azat river gorge

Aragats mountain

Mountain Azhdahak

Culture Language Alphabet Literature

Mesrop Mashtots

Being one of the most ancient of existing languages, Armenian (hayeren) belongs to the eastern group of the Indo–European linguistic family with certain similarities to paleobalcanic languages and the Greek. However, it forms an independent branch. A new phase of development found its way with the creation of the Alphabet in 405. Being composed of 36 letters, the Armenian alphabet was created by the scientist, monk Mesrop Mashtots under the harsh politico–economic conditions of that period. It aspired to attract more believers towards the church, offering them a possibility of liturgy in Armenian thanks to the translation of the Bible into Armenian. In the Late Middle Ages, in the XII century, two letters were added to the alphabet. In the XX century one more letter joined the family and

Matenadaran

ARMENIAN ALPHABET

Ա ա	[a] 1	Ժ ժ	[zh] 10	Ճ ճ	[tch] 100	Ռ ռ	[rr] 1000
Բ բ	[b] 2	Ի ի	[i] 20	Մ մ	[m] 200	Ս ս	[s] 2000
Գ գ	[gu] 3	Լ լ	[l] 30	Յ յ	[y] 300	Վ վ	[v] 3000
Դ դ	[d] 4	Խ խ	[j] 40	Ն ն	[n] 400	Տ տ	[t] 4000
Ե ե	[ye] 5	Ծ ծ	[ts] 50	Շ շ	[sh] 500	Ր ր	[r] 5000
Զ զ	[z] 6	Կ կ	[k] 60	Ո ո	[o] 600	Ց ց	[ts] 6000
Է է	[ē] 7	Հ հ	[h] 70	Չ չ	[ch] 700	Ու ու	[u] 7000
Ը ը	[ĕ] 8	Ձ ձ	[dz] 80	Պ պ	[p] 800	Փ փ	[p'] 8000
Թ թ	[th] 9	Ղ ղ	[gh] 90	Ջ ջ	[dj] 900	Ք ք	[q] 9000

Hovhannes Tumanyan

formed the current Armenian alphabet of 39 letters.

36 letters, created by Mashtots, served as figures until the XVI century; divided into 4 columns, 9 letters in each. The first column was equivalent to units, the second one to ten(s), the third one to hundred(s) and the last one to thousand(s).

With the creation of the Alphabet the Golden Age for Armenian literature was initiated. The first translation done into Armenian was that of the Bible, which Mashtots translated himself from Greek. The first literature work was written by Koryun in 440 and was called "The life of Mashtots". During the same century historiography, hymnography and hagiography started to prosper. In the VI century Armenian philosophy reached new levels, thanks to the work of David Anhaght (Invincible). The first examples of laic poetry from the VII century have survived to this day. The definite liberation from the Arab yoke in the end of the IX century opened a new phase in Armenian literature: the Renaissance. First and foremost this period is related to the name of the prominent Armenian poet Grigor Narekatsi. In the XI century the formation of the Medieval Armenian began. In the XIII century Armenian was used by the founder of social protest, poet Frik, and by the founder of Armenian poetry Yerznkatsi. The establishment of the principality, later the kingdom of Cilicia in 1080 played an important role in this process.

Among the writers and poets of the XIX century the names of Khachatur Abovyan, Hovhannes Tumanyan, Raffi, Alexander Shirvanzade and others are

Yeghishe Charents

worth mentioning. On the one hand, the Soviet period was characterized by literature prosperity. On the other hand, it was an era of censorship by the party. Among poets and writers both accepted and not accepted by the Government are Yeghishe Charents, Paruyr Sevak, Hovhannes Shiraz and alike. One of the well–known Diaspora writers is William Saroyan. The archaic language, called "grabar", nowadays is used only during the liturgy, while the modern one has two important divisions of the Western Armenian, used by the Diaspora and the Eastern Armenian, spoken in the Republic of Armenia and in the Armenian communities of Russia, Georgia and Iran.

William Saroyan

Music

Komitas

Aram Khachatryan

One may find references to the examples of pre–Christian music in the works of ancient Armenian authors. This is very much linked to the work of "gusans" (troubadour) who served in the temple of God of the Armenian mythology Gisane during the Hellenistic era. Armenian Christian music, together with the Aramean and Jewish ones, form the basis of Christian musical culture. In the V century Mesrop Mashtots created the first collection of "sharakans" (religious songs). In the Middle Ages the theory of acoustics was elaborated in Armenia. During the VII–IX centuries a new system of Armenian musical notes was created. It was called "khazer" and came to substitute the letters. During the second half of the XVI century the art of Armenian "ashughs" (singer–poet) was established. Among them the most prominent ones were Naghash Hovnatan and Sayat Nova. In 1868 Tigran Chukhajyan composed the first Armenian national opera "Arshak II". In the end of the XIX century a new phase began in the Armenian national music: a new movement of collecting the ancient Armenian folklore music by professional composers. The biggest contribution was made by the greatest Armenian composer Komitas. In the beginning of the XX century Alexander Spendiaryan and Armen Tigranyan caught the eye for their outstanding musical pieces. The latter finished his famous "Anush' opera in 1912. One of the Armenian composers known all over the world is Aram Khachaturyan, the author of ballets "Gayane" and "Spartak". National musical instruments are: thar, saz, kamancha, kanon, duduk (Armenian national flute).

Duduk, included in UNESCO intangible heritage list

Miniature

Out of 25 thousand Armenian medieval miniatures 10 thousand are illustrated; 5–7 of them are whole miniatures. More frequently the Gospels, more rarely the Bibles, "tonakanner" and "chashotsner" were illustrated. The most ancient preserved miniatures date back to the VI–VII centuries, being wonderful samples of the Early Christianity art. The miniatures of that era are thematic: until the first half of the XI century miniatures were painted on the cover page of the manuscript. The miniatures of that era are linear, made of watercolor touches and with simple ribbons. Every Gospel starts with an image of the Evangelist, who is almost always painted in a sitting position. During the second half of the XII century the art of illustrating the "tonakanner" (religious collection) was formed. In these manuscripts the text starts with an image of the protagonist or the author with a decorated initial letter and "glkhazard".

The Armenian miniature has the following main groups and phases of development: miniatures before the XI century, the schools of Greater and Lesser Armenia of the XI–XII centuries, the school of the XII–XIV centuries of Cilician Armenia, the schools of Bardzr Hayk, Ani, Artsakh, Gladzor, Tatev and Vaspurakan from the XII century.

Armenian manuscript

Cochineal

The Armenian cochineal or the cochineal of Ararat is an insect type from hemiptera family. Red dye known in Armenian as "vordan karmir" is obtained from female cochineal. A huge number of Armenian medieval miniatures were painted with this dye. Moreover, the wool, that was used to tile the famous Armenian carpets, was colored with cochineal as well. It has been proven that the wool of the most ancient world carpet of Pazyryk (V century BC, currently in Hermitage, St. Petersburg) was also colored with the Armenian cochineal.

Painting

The XVIII–XIX centuries marked a new period for Armenian art full of new ideas. Hakob Hovnatanyan, whose gallery of portraits opened a new page in the development of national painting, is a fine example of this process. The influence of European painting is significant. Because of the unfavorable political and economic conditions in Armenia, the Armenian painters were predominantly engaged in artistic activity in Tiflis (Tbilisi), St. Petersburg and Moscow, as well

as in the cities of Western and Eastern Europe. In the 1880s a whole pleiad of remarkable artists emerged, whose works were dedicated to the national theme. This genre, however, reached its apogee in the work of one of the greatest Armenian painters, Vardges Surenyants, who was creating at the turn of the XIX-XX centuries. In the 1890s the landscape painting was formed as an independent branch in the Armenian painting. Gevorg Bashinjaghyan became the founder of the professional landscape painting. The works of the most prominent Armenian painters of the XIX century, such as the invincible master of etching Edgar Shahin, the great marine artist Hovhannes Ayvazovski should definitely be mentioned.

Martiros Saryan

The regions of Armenia and their places of interest

Shirak region

Distance:	126 km northwest from Yerevan to Gyumri
Population:	280 thousand inhabitants
Centre:	Gyumri (146 thousand inhabitants)
Number of cities:	3 (Gyumri, Artik, Maralik)
Number of villages:	107
Altitude:	1500–2000m above sea level
Monasteries and churches:	*Marmashen, Haritchavank, Yereruyk, Lmbatavank, Artik, Yoth Verq, Pemzashen*

Shirak region borders Georgia in the North and Turkey in the West. In the South and Southeast it borders Aragatsotn region and in the East and Northeast Lori region. Ashotsk plateau is located in Shirak region. Its height reaches 1800-2200m above sea level. The absolute minimum temperature is –46°C. This is the coldest area of the Republic, "the Pole of cold", as it is usually called. The only large river of the region is Akhuryan, which originates from Lake Arpi. Akhuryan deposit, which is the largest in the Republic, was constructed on the river.

The region got devastated because of the horrible earthquakes of the past century in 1926 and in 1988. The latter almost entirely demolished the city of Gyumri, caused thousands of casualties, destroyed factories and companies. A lot of families left the city: from 230 thousand inhabitants living there during the 80s, nowadays only 146 thousand people remain

Gyumri

in Gyumri. However, it is still the second biggest city in the country. The reconstruction activity within the city is still ongoing. Monument of Charles Aznavour, the greatest Armenian patron, stands in the city center. Before Independence the city was called Leninakan.

Marmashen Monastery

Marmashen Monastery is situated 2km northwest of Marmashen village, on the bank of the river Akhuryan (on the Turkish border). According to the inscription carved on the southern wall of the principal church of St. Katoghike it was constructed during 988–1029 by the prince Vahram Pahlavuni. The dome occupies the central position of the exterior volume. The eastern altar, similar to that of the cathedral in Ani, is decorated with niches intended for frescos. The second church is located north of the principal church. It was probably constructed during the same period and represents a small imitation of the main church; currently it is in ruins. The Prince Pahlavuni's grave is located there. Southwest of the atrium there are the ruins of a circular church. The small Marmashen is situated on the hill north of the monastic complex.

Artik

The small church of Marine or Holy Virgin of the IV–V centuries (currently in ruins) presents a great value for the Armenian architecture. This is an example of transition from basilica to domed basilica. Similar to Mastara churches, St. Gregory church of Artik dates back to the VII century.

Haritchavank

The most ancient construction of the complex is St. Gregory church of the VII century; the lateral altars adjacent from the south are from the XIII century. The main church was constructed in 1201 by the request of Zakaryan brothers. It is a cruciform domical church. The image on the upper part of eastern façade presenting a cross that forms a circle with a relief of Zakaryan brothers is quite extraordinary. A "fan–shaped" dome crowns the church. South of the principal church stands an atrium (gavit) of a bit asymmetric shape from the XIII century. The decoration of the lintel of the atrium is amazing. In the southern part of the village there is an area from the Bronze Age with a surface of 12 ha, where different artifacts dating back to the III millennium B.C. were found.

Lmbatavank

Lmbatavank is located 2km southwest of the town of Artik. The church of St. Stephanos (Stephen), approximately of the VI century, is a small cruciform church both from inside and outside. According to the inscriptions, the dome was reconstructed in the X century. On the main apse pieces of frescos from the VII century can be found.

Saint Sign (Surb Nshan) or Seven Wounds

The church is located in the center of Gyumri. It was constructed in 1859. Primarily, it was called Surb Astvatsatsin (Cathedral of the Holy Mother of God), but among people it is known as "Yoth Verq" (Seven Wounds). Next to the church there are two domes that fell down during the 1988 earthquake.

Pemzashen

In the center of Pemzashen village a monastic complex from the early Middle Ages is located. It is comprised of a single–nave basilica (V century; only the bases have been preserved) and another single–nave church without a dome (VI century) in the South. Between these two a cruciform domical church (VI century) can be seen. There is a carving of St. Mary holding the baby and angels above them on the western façade of the tympanum.

Southeast of Pemzashen, on the way towards the village Lernakert, Saint Sion church constructed in 1001 is located. Around the church there is an old cemetery. In the nearby gorge one may see a single–nave church of Surb Astvatsatsin (Holy Mother of God) from the XVII century. The only preserved church of the XI century in Arakelots monastery (Apostles) is in Pemzashen territory. The rest of the constructions of the monastery are in ruins. West of the monastery is the tomb of Vahram Pahlavuni's brother with a cross stone from 1036. The Bronze Age objects, dating back to II millennium BC, were encountered in Pemzashen area.

Yereruyk

Next to the Anipemza village Yereruyk basilica (IV–V century), one of the biggest and the most ancient buildings of the early Christianity, is situated. Currently it is in ruins. This is a construction of three naves and six columns standing on a stylobate (basis of the steps). The central nave is three times wider than the lateral ones. In the western part is the atrium gallery of three arches (the result of reconstruction) that ruined the western pediment (frontal). The lateral altars on both sides of the eastern apse, as well as four altars of two floors in the west are annexed. The tympanum, the door, the window frames and the capital of the basilica are illustrated with impressive ornamental decorations. Diverse ruins were found in the surroundings of the basilica. Underground halls with chimneys reaching the surface were discovered. Its functions are still unknown. Close to the basilica there is a children cemetery. According to archaeologists it dates back to the V–VI centuries. Presumably, the children, who died without being baptized, were buried there next to the basilica dedicated to John the Baptist.

Tavush region

Distance:	136km northeast from Yerevan to Ijevan
Population:	135 thousand inhabitants
Centre:	Ijevan (20 thousand inhabitants)
Number of cities:	5 (Ijevan, Dilijan, Ayrum, Berd, Noyemberyan)
Number of villages:	62
Altitude:	the highest mountain Murghuz — 2993m
Monasteries and churches:	*Goshavank, Haghartsin, Makaravank, Kaptavank, Dzukhtak, Mshkavanq, Atcharkut, Arakelots, Deghdznut, Kirants, Navur, Nor Varagavank, Shjmuradi, Voskepar, Srvegh, Gosh lake, Lastiver, Samson*
Fortresses:	*Tavush, Berdavan*
Landscape:	*National park of Dilijan, Kirants Samsoni gorge*

Tavush region borders the regions of Gegharkunik and Kotayk in the South and Southeast, Lori in the West, Georgia in the West and Azerbaijan in the East and Northeast. The frontier with the latter is 300km long. The lowest point of the Armenian relief (380m) is in the North of the region, close to Debedavan village. The highest point of the region is Murghuz of Miaphor mountain range. It is typical for the mountains of the region to have rocky slopes and gorges covered with forests of 200–600m in depth. The climate is moderate; the average temperature in January varies from O°C to –8°C and can reach +12 +22°C in July. The annual amount of precipitation is 500–600mm. The climate in the mountainous South and valleys in the North differs a lot. The main rivers of the region are Aghstev, Debed, Hakhum, Tavush.

Yenokavan

Lastiver

Lastiver is situated in the north-east of Armenia, three km from the village of Yenokavan. Touristic route starts from the Yenokavan village resort area and continues along the gorge of the river Khachaghbyur, going deep into the forest. Soon a breathtaking view opens before you-two beautiful waterfalls. But the most exciting sight is still ahead, that is Lastiver caves. It is known that local inhabitants used to hide and pray in those caves during the Mongol invasion in the XIII-XIV centuries. The cave is situated on the vertical slope of the gorge and it is not so easy to get there. There are numerous bas-reliefs on the walls of the rooms among which there is one depicting a woman, cut by sculptor B. Poghosyan in 1970. Not far from Yenokavan village, there is a great place for fans of extreme rest - a zip-line that contains 5 lines.

Lake Parz

20km east of Dilijan at the height of 1334m above sea level, Lake Parz, one of the favorite places of the holidaymakers, is located. It is surrounded by mountains covered with thick forests. 2.2km southwest of village Gosh one can see Lake Gosh, which is much smaller, but it is located in the center of a forest similar to Lake Parz.

Dilijan is also known as "Little Switzerland" due to its mountainous green landscape that reigns in this territory. Being rich in mineral and thermal springs Dilijan has many great health resorts.

Little Armenian Switzerland

The flora and fauna of Tavush region is very rich. Here the National Dilijan Park and Ijevan arboretum are located. The core variety of natural forests includes oak, oriental beech, white beech, maple, linden, pine. Among fauna species one can encounter chamois, Caucasian bear, wild boar, hare, fox, lynx, hedgehog, squirrel. A wide diversity of fish, including brown trout can be seen in rivers.

The avenues of yew trees, the largest of them (25 ha) close to Aghavnavank village, are of great interest. There are 700 varieties of exotic plants in Ijevan arboretum.

Mshkavank

It is located near Koghb village. The church of Surb Astvatsatsin (Holy Mother of God) and the atrium (gavit) have been preserved. The exact date of the construction is unknown. It is mentioned that the church was built in 1219.

It consists of a square, single–nave hall. On the eastern façade, on top of the window, a carving of a cross with a bullhead above is visible. The only entrance of the church leads to an atrium, which has a prolonged shape. The buildings were under restoration during 1955–1960.

Arakelots

3 km west of village Kirants the medieval monastery called Arakelots (Apostles) is situated. The monastery encompasses two churches, atrium and administrative buildings.

The main church (XIII century) belongs to a domed-hall type of churches. The small church is a single–nave basilica.

Goshavank

Goshavank monastic complex (XII–XIII century) is located in Gosh village. It has been a very important religious, educational and cultural center.

In 1188 Mkhitar Gosh, the famous scholar and the author of the first Armenian Code of Laws, with the support of the prince Zakaryan built the current complex in the place of the monastery destroyed by an earthquake.

The main church of Surb Astvatsatsin (Holy Mother of God, 1191–1196) has domed halls with two entrances: western and northern. The atrium (gavit) from 1197–1203 belongs to the type of central domed structures supported by four columns. It has lateral altars of two floors in eastern corners. South of the atrium the chapel of Gregory the Illuminator (from 1231) can be found, which is a domeless basilica. Despite its small size it catches an eye with its stone decoration.

St. Gregory the Illuminator church (finished in 1231) is located south of the main one. Its dome has not survived. According to historical records, master Mkhitar called "Hyusn" carried out these constructions. North of the atrium a library (1241) is situated. A bell tower was added to it in 1291. The bases of the library and the walls of the academy that connect it to the western one are made of plain stone roofed with wooden beams.

In the southern part, not far from the monastery, St. George church (1254), the ruins of the house pertaining to Mkhitar Gosh, as well as his mausoleum are situated.

Code of Laws

The prominent intellectual, statesman and theologian Mkhitar Gosh compiled the first Armenian secular code of laws in 1184. It consists of three main parts: prologue, ecclesiastical laws and secular laws. Some points of the "Code of Laws" are striking because of the author's perverse sense of justice, for example, Article 105 "Shipwrecks at sea". In those times there was a law over coastal zones according to which any ship and its cargo became the property of the coastal zone owner of the country where the ship wrecked. Mkhitar Gosh was the first in the Armenian legislation to reject this law and in Article 105 stated that if this kind of accident happened at the Armenian coasts both the ship and its cargo were to be returned to the owner. And the rescuers had the right to get remuneration constituting one tenth or one fifth of the salvaged property. A similar law was adopted in Europe, particularly in France, only 500 years later. Gosh demanded that the workers should be paid on the same day before sunset, suggesting the following as the support of his claims: "It is clear that he has to work because of his current need for money". Gosh established equality between spouses in the disposition of matrimonial property. We can conclude that Gosh aspired to very noble objectives, that is to protect women's property and honor, as well as strengthen family and reduce the number of frivolous divorces by means of legal norms.

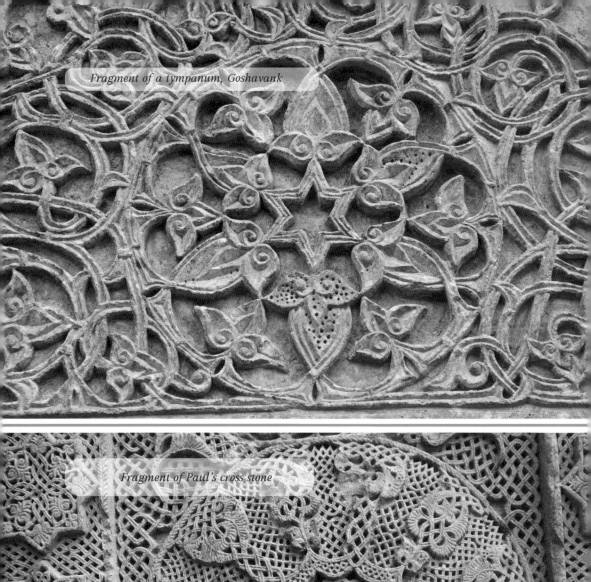

Fragment of a tympanum, Goshavank

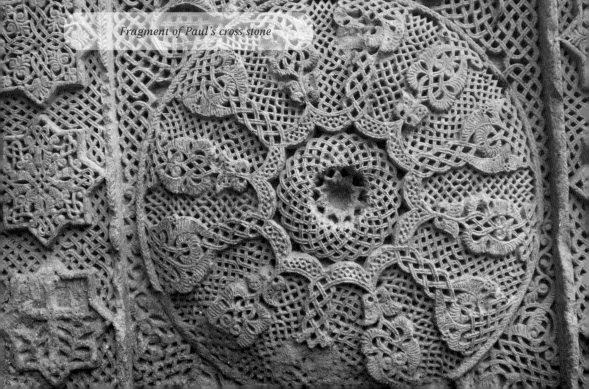

Fragment of Paul's cross stone

Haghartsin

Haghartsin monastery is situated 18km north of Dilijan in a dense forest. It is currently under the patronage of Dilijan National Park.

The monastic complex comprises three churches, two atriums (one is in ruins), refectory, several chapels, kitchen (in ruins), bakery and cross stones. The most ancient church is that of St.Gregory (X century). It is a domed cruciform construction. Lateral altars are located in the corners. The atrium (gavit) is situated west of the church.

Ivane Zakaryan built it in the beginning of the XIII century. It is a four–column construction the plane roofs of which have various bas–reliefs with images of humans, birds, angels and rose windows in the corners.

St. Stephen's (1244) and St. Gregory's churches are located north and east of the chapel respectively. They are made of bluish basalt with tiny precious details. The main church of Surb Astvatsatsin (Holy Mother of God) is a domed hall.

According to the inscription of the southern façade it was built in 1281. However, it is believed

that this is the date of the reconstruction of the church in X–XI centuries. West of the church the ruins of an atrium have been preserved.

A refectory built in 1248 is located in the western part of the complex. In accordance with the inscription on the southwest sentrance Minas was the architect, who constructed it. There are only two refectories with such an architectural solution. The second one is in Haghpat. This is a large hall with two domes that rest upon two central columns and the lateral ones and four intersecting arches located below each dome. In the South the refectory is connected with the kitchen (currently in ruins) thanks to the second door, which is much wider. East of the refectory the bakery has been preserved.

Currently the monastery is restored thanks to the grants from Pan–Armenian Hayastan foundation and the support of the sheikh Sultan bin Mohamed Al-Qasimi.

Dilijan

Makaravank

The monastery is situated 3km southwest of Achajur village on the slope of Paytathap Mountain. The main church was built in 1205. From outside it has a rectangular shape, from inside it is a cruciform of a domed composition made of pink andesite. Eastern and southern façades are decorated with triangle niches; the tambour of the dome is decorated with a two-column arcade. The western portal has a very peculiar decoration. Almost the same decoration can be found on the northern porch ending in the atrium. On the eastern façade of the church there is a high relief with an eagle holding a ram in his talons. The decoration of the altar stands out as well. Its façade is entirely covered with carved eight–tips stars. Various images of flora and fauna are represented within their rosettes (the fish and the architect are perfect). This ornament is one of the masterpieces of the medieval
Armenian art. The bas–reliefs of the fish images with their expressiveness and realistic style are one of a kind. The image of the architect is carved with his tools and name "Young" on one of the stars. The second church of Makaravank (X–XI centuries) is Northeast of the complex. The major elements for the decoration of the church are the refined geometrical and floral ornaments of the façade of the altar that probably served as a prototype for the major church. The atrium (1207), which is connected to the ancient church in the East and with the main one in the South, is almost square: a centered composition with 4 columns. In the West on top of the principal entrance there are high reliefs presenting a scenery of a fight between a lion, a bull and a spirit.

In the eastern part of the complex you can see Surb Astvatsatsin (Holy Mother of God) church, built by Hovhannes, the head of the diocese of the monastery in 1198. Externally the composition is octahedral and internally it is cruciform. Additionally, it has rich external decorations: rosettes, birds, lions, a fight between an eagle and a dragon. In its North a small chapel is situated. Makaravank with its high and bas–reliefs occupies a significant and special place in Armenian art and architecture.

Lori region

Distance:	116km northeast from Yerevan to Vanadzor
Population:	282 thousand inhabitants
Centre:	Vanadzor (104 thousand inhabitants)
Number of cities:	8
	(Vanadzor, Spitak, Stepanavan, Alaverdi, Tashir, Akhtala, Tumanyan, Shamlugh)
Number of villages:	122
The highest mountain:	Tezh 3110m
Monasteries and churches:	*Sanahin, Haghpat, Akhtala, Odzun, Kobayr, Hnevank, Khutchap, Kurtan, Horomayr, Dzgrashen, St. Gregory Barzraqash, Ardvi, Khorakert, Qaranist Mankants, Tormakavank, Manstev, Sedvi, Shnogh, Dorband*
Fortresses:	*Lori Berd, Kayanberd*
Landscape:	*Stepanavan arboretum*

Lori region borders Georgia in the North, Shirak region in the Northwest, Tavush region in the East, Aragatsotn and Gegharkunik regions in the South. The typical landscape of Lori presents extensive mountain ranges with pre–alpine vegetation, deep gorges, layered slopes and rugged hillsides. The largest rivers are Debed and its tributaries Dzoraget, Marts and Pambak. The region is rich in minerals. The climate is mild and humid.

Vanadzor

The center of the region is Vanadzor (Kirovakan before the Independence, Gharakilisa prior the Bolsheviks' arrival). In the 1950s it was converted into a big industrial center. Currently, it is the third city of the Republic in terms of population.

Stepanavan arboretum

It has a territory of 35 ha, 17,5 of which is the natural forest and 15 ha includes decorative trees. Edmon Leonowich, who was the director of the place up to 1984, founded the arboretum in 1931. During the existence of the arboretum 2500 species of plants were planted. However, only 500 species managed to adapt to the climate conditions.

Hnevank

Hnevank monastery (VII century) is located east of Kurtan village where Dzoraget and Gargar rivers meet. From outside it has a rectangular shape; from inside it consists of three apses with a lateral altar in the corners. According to the inscription on the tambour of 1144 the church was built by prince Smbat Orbelyan. The atrium (gavit) was constructed in 1186–1206, as stated in the inscription on the portico. In 2006 restoration work commenced. Only two rows of the wall stones from another single–nave church were preserved. Economic structures are situated on the western and eastern sides of the complex.

Sanahin

It is in the UNESCO World Heritage list. Sanahin monastic complex was founded by the Bagratid king Ashot the Compassionate in 966. It was declared the Heritage of Humanity in 1996, together with Haghpat monastery next to it. Literally, the word Sanahin is translated from Armenian as "this is much older than that one", which presumably indicates that this church was built earlier than the neighboring Haghpat monastery.

The monastery had an increasing cultural importance; humanities, medicine and other sciences were taught here. It also had a library from where a plethora of precious manuscripts were kept; the majority of them were illustrated with miniatures.

The monastic complex is centered next to the church of Mother of God. They started building it in 930 and finished only ten years later. It has a nave with a transept and four annexed lateral altars. The queen Khosrovanuysh and her husband Ashot III built the church of St. Savour during 966–972. This is the most important church of the monastery and it is dedicated to

their sons Smbat and Grigor, who are pictured on the high relief of the eastern façade with the model of the church in their hands. The dome was redone in 1184. Between these two churches there was a theological school (X century) fwhere the Armenian scholar and philosopher Mkhitar Pahlavuni taught for many years.

The atrium (gavit) of St. Savour church was built in 1181. It is a pioneer example of a building type with four central columns and a semi–spherical dome. Prince Vache Vachutyan built the atrium of the church of the Mother of God church in 1211. It differs greatly from others: it is a triple–nave hall separated by the columns covered with barrel vault. North of the atrium there is a bell tower from the XIII century. East of the bell tower there is a valuable library from the XI century, in front of which one can find a gallery from the XIII century. The mausoleum of Zakaryan (Zakarids) dynasty stands isolated nearby. The church of Resurrection (Harutyun) from the XII century, St. Jacob church from the X century and the refectory reformed and reutilized by the Soviets are in the territory of the complex.

Haghpat

Haghpat monastery was founded by the Bagratid queen Khosrovanuysh and king Ashot III the Compassionate (Voghormats). The neighboring Sanahin monastery was built during the same period.

The name Haghpat comes from the words "haghb", which means strong and "pat", which means wall. In 1996 it was included in the UNESCO World Heritage list.

The biggest church of the complex, the cathedral of St. Sign (Surb Nshan), was constructed in 976 and it is a typical example of Armenian architecture of the X century.

Its central dome rests upon four impressive pillars of the lateral walls. External walls hang on triangle holes. A fresco on the apse represents the Christ Pantocrator.

The sons of the church founders, princes Smbat and Gurgen, are also depicted on the high relief of eastern façade. In the beginning of the XIII century an atrium (gavit) was added to the main church. The atrium has an extremely curious interior structure.

Northeast of the main church there is the chapel of Mother of God (Surb Astvatsatsin) from the XII century. Southwest the XI century St. Gregory church is situated.

To the north of the main church is "The house of Hamazasp", which is the biggest atrium of Armenia constructed by monastery's superior father Hamazasp in 1257.

In 1245 the three–floor bell tower was built. In 1248 a refectory, situated northeast of the church, was added. It is a hall with two domes resting upon two central and lateral columns; from the latter four arches intersect below every dome.

The library from the XI century is united with the northern part of the eastern wall of "the house of Hamazasp". The library was entirely reconstructed in the XIII century. Inside the library one may get surprised at finding large earthenware jars.

It turns out that the libraries, both in Sanahin and Haghpat, served as warehouses, and the nuns used to keep the provisions in those jars.

A series of amazing cross stones (khachkars) from XI–XIII centuries can be seen in the territory of the monastery. Among them the most well known is the one called "the Savour" (Amenaprkich) from 1273. There are also cross stones from the mausoleum of Uqanants family (XIII) and many more.

The monastery has been damaged many times. However, the majority of the complex managed to avoid substantial alterations.

Akhtala frescos

Akhtala

Between 1887 and 1889 French archaeologist Jacques de Morgan discovered 576 rectangular stone sepulchers along with other clerical objects of bronze and iron dating back to the VIII century in Akhtala.

The first constructions in the area began during the Bronze and Iron Ages, though the fort was built at the end of X century (by the Kyurikyan family during the period of Lori Kingdom).

Akhtala became a fortified monastery in the X century. It is located in Akhtala village.

The fort played an important role in defending the Northwest of Armenia, the region previously called Gugarq. Furthermore, this construction is considered to be one of the most well–preserved ones in the country.

The main church is famous for its high artistic quality frescos that cover its interior walls. It is believed that the current name derives from Turkish.

Since the XVIII century the Greek ethnic groups established in Akhtala have been using the monastery for gold and silver mines exploitation. Approximately 800 Greek families moved from Gümüşhene during the rule of the Ottoman Empire in 1763.

The Greeks called the monastery Meramani and left inscriptions on its walls. In the XIX century the noble Melikov family owned Akhtala.

Odzun

According to the tradition in the I century the apostle Thomas came to the village and consecrated priests and bishops where church now stands. The name of the village Odzun comes from the word "consecrate", which in Armenian sounds like "odzel".

Apostle Thomas brought with him the blanket (manta) of baby Jesus, which is buried under the altar of the current church. Above the southern entrance of the church an inscription was preserved. In the IV century a basilica of St.Gregory the Illuminator was constructed here. However, an earthquake destroyed it in the V century.

The current church was built in the VI century. The latter is a triple–nave domed basilica using more than 20 reliefs from the basilica of the IV century. The roof of the church was repaired in the XIX century.

In the 80s of the last century the restoration work began. With this aim they took down three columns of the northern gallery. However, after the collapse of the USSR the work stopped.

Ten meters northeast of the church is the IV century obelisk with two carved steles.

In 2013 restoration activity of the church resumed. Previously, the church was linked to the church Tsiranavor (V century), which is 1.5km away, with an underground exit door.

Kobayr

Kobayr is the monastic complex from XII–XIII centuries built by the Kyurikyan family and later by the Georgian representatives of the Zakarids. It "is hanging" at 150m height on the very sharp slope of the rock (though it is visible from the road, there is no car access there). It is comprised of 4 churches, a bell tower, a refectory and a domed hall (the majority is in ruins). It stands out due to its incomparable frescos that survived in the main church and some of the chapels. There are many great inscriptions in a chronological order both in Armenian and Georgian on the walls.

Khutchapi vank

Khutchap monastery is on the northern slope of the mountain Lalvar. The most ancient structure is a single–nave church of the IX–X centuries. Khutchap monastery was first mentioned as a convent. During the Zakarids reign in the XIII century it was turned into a monastery. In the same century the major church with rich exterior decorations was built. The remnants of frescos are preserved in the lateral southern altar. The atrium (gavit) is in the western part of the main church. Large halls were added in northern and southern parts. Together with the XII century construction, the basilica was renovated. North of the basilica a dilapidated chapel can be seen. Some administrative constructions and a prison were preserved in the fortified zone of the monastery.

Lori fortress

Lori berd medieval fortress ("berd" is translated as a fortress) is 4.5km from Stepanavan, on the crossroad of Dzoraget and Urut. It was built approximately in 1005–1020 by David Anhogh ("without a land").

The town fortress was the capital of Kyurikyan kingdom occupying 35ha and having 10 thousand inhabitants during the XI–XIII centuries. During its history it belonged to the Zakarids, the Orbelyans, Turks, Persians and Georgians. A church and two baths are preserved on the territory of the fortress. A medieval round bridge is located on the downhill next to the fortress.

Ardvi

Ardvi village is situated 5km away from Odzun and is known for the monastery of St. John Odznetsi (718–728), which is located northwest of the village. The church was built of big and irregular stones. There is a bell tower next to the church. The history of the church is closely related to that of Catholicos Hovhannes Odznetsi. In 1902 Meliq Kalantaryan reconstructed the church. Here one may also encounter the famous "Snake navel" spring ("odzi port" in Armenian). According to the legend a woman sees a snake and begins calling for help. Hovhannes Odznetsi sends his seven pupils. None of them returns. Then he goes himself. He touches the snake with his stick and tells him: "Let healing water come out from your navel while you turn into a stone". According to the Institute of Geology tests' results the water of the spring contains gold and silver.

Sanahin bridge

Sanahin bridge, situated on the river Debed in the city of Alaverdi, is a very important construction of Armenian medieval engineering, dating back to the end of the XII century.

Among the ancient bridges this is the most well-preserved one. Its span reaches 18.6m in height. The bridge was built by Vaneni, the sister of princes Zakare and Ivane.

Several flats of stairs connect lower levels of Sanahin bridge with the main horizontal level. In four corners of the central pillar four lions are pictured as protective symbols.

The Molokons

One of the minority groups of the country, the community of the molokons, lives in this region. Their name derives from the Russian word "moloko"(milk). This name is used due to the fact that these people, including the days of the fest, consume milk against religious inscriptions. Moreover, the molokons explain their own doctrine: "Our milk is spiritual". Pertaining to spiritual Christians, they have become the center of attention not only for their honesty and hard work, but also for their religious customs. They do reject many established religious rituals: do not recognize the worship of icons and temples, accept the authority of neither priests nor other high church officials. They are skeptical about canonization of any person. They prefer to communicate with God from their houses during praying hours. The molokons are considered to be peaceful people; that are not even allowed to touch a weapon. They have abstemious lifestyle. The most important thing for them is to do good in consonance with Christian norms. In the second half of the XVIII century their members

began uniting in big communities in the central and southern regions of Russia. Afterwards they were persecuted and exiled from Russia. In Armenia they mainly live in the villages of Fioletovo, Margahovit and Lermontovo. They do not live isolated there are also Armenians living in those villages.

Dsegh

After crossing the Pambak river by a bridge and diverting from the main road, one stumbles upon Dsegh village, one of the most ancient inhabited areas in Armenia. This is the birthplace of one of the greatest Armenian writers Hovhannes Tumanyan (1869–1923). His house museum is also situated right here. The village is also famous for the great amount of churches, chapels, cross stones (khachkars), among which the basilica from 654 built by Mamikonyan princes, St. Gregory monastery (XII–XIII), the monastery of Forty Children (Qarasun Mankots, XII century) stand out.

Aragatsotn region

Distance:	22km northwest from Yerevan to Ashtarak
Centre:	Ashtarak city (21 thousand inhabitants)
Number of cities:	3
	(Ashtarak, Aparan, Talin)
Number of villages:	117
Population:	142 thousand inhabitants
The highest mountain:	Aragats (4090m)
Monasteries and churches:	Saghmosavank, Hovhanavank, Aruch, Tegher, Oshakan,Ushi, Mughni, Katoghike of Talin, Mastara, Karmravor, Tsiranavor, Dashtadem, Astvatsnkal, Artavazik, Karbi, Kosh, Marine, Nerseh Kamsarakan, Voskevaz
Other places of interest:	Byurakan observatory, Aghts mausoleum
Fortresses:	Amberd, Kagheni, Shamiram
Landscape:	Mountain Aragats, Lake Kari

Aragatsotn region borders Yerevan in the Southeast, Armavir in the south, Shirak in the Northwest, Lori in the north, Kotayk in the East and Northeast and Turkey in the West.

Mount Aragats

The main river of the region is Kasakh and its tributaries Amberd and Gegharot. The water deposit of Aparan is located on the river Kasakh.

The climate is varied because of height differences. For instance, if in the lower area summer lasts for 5 months (May–September), in the area of mountain Aragats the major part of the year is winter; it is possible to see snow on top of the mountain.

Lake Kari is located on the slopes of mountain Ararat, with 3207m above sea level, 0.12km^2 surface and 9m in depth. In higher areas of the mountain one may see alpine and pre–alpine meadows that are often interrupted with rocky slopes and small oak forests.

On the slope of mountain Aragats Byurakan observatory is situated, founded and managed for a long period of time by the renowned scientist Viktor Hambardzumyan.

Vahramashen church, Amberd

Amberd fortress

The medieval town–fortress of Amberd was built in the X century and is located 7km North of the city of Byurakan on the slopes of Mountain Aragats. It is situated on a triangular basis formed by the gorges of the rivers Amberd and Arqashen at 2300m above sea level. The castle and part of the wall were built in the VII century.

Since the X century it belonged to Pahlavuni princes and was one of the most strategically important bastions of the Bagratid dynasty. It was invaded by Seljuks in the XI and by Mongols in the XII century.

In the following century (XIII) the prince Vachutyan reconstructed Amberd. The ruins of the castle, remnants of the walls of the fortress, the church (1026), the bath and fragments of other constructions have been preserved up to now. Inside the castle and fortress there are ruins of water depositories. The fortress also has a secret exit.

Yazidis

Yazidi form a pre–Islamic minority, which originated back in 2000 B.C. Once it was the official religion of Kurds as well, but the obligatory islamization reduced its numbers. Nevertheless, they are still predominantly of Kurdish origin; before the dramatic events in 2014 the majority of them were living close to Mosul (Iraq), with small communities living in Armenia, Georgia, Iran, Russia, Syria and Turkey. Yazidis speak in Kurmanji language. Their religion, Yezidism, is mostly based on oral traditions. They also have two sacred books with dogmas, laws, cosmogony and rituals. The main cult and the central figure of faith is Melek Taus, or the Peacock Angel. Traditionally, the Yazidi society is divided into 2 endogamic groups; religious and laic ones. The minority group of Yazidi is mainly concentrated in Aragatsotn region. Since the 1990s "the Voice of Yazidis" ('Dange Yezdya") newspaper has been published. Armenian nation highly appreciates the assistance of Yazidis in the heroic battle of Sardarapat in 1918.

Hovhanavank

Hovhanavank monastery is located in Ohanavan village on the edge of a splendid gorge of the river Kasakh. Ruins of the IV century church, which was probably built instead of a pagan temple, can be found in the territory of Hovhanavank complex. In the East there are remnants of the most ancient church of the complex, which is a single–nave basilica from the V century. In the XIII century by the order of the prince Vache Vachutyan the main church was constructed in the southern part of the basilica.

A bit later, commissioned by his son, the atrium (1250) connected to both churches was built. The atrium is spacious; its central part is crowned with a round bell tower of 12 sides with 6.5 m in diameter. The decorations of both western façade of the atrium and western façade of the major church are peculiar: braided octagons and a bas–relief representing the parable of "wise and foolish virgins" are carved on the lintel.

On the right side of the main altar behind the lateral one a secret exit can be found. According to the legend it saved the lives of the village people. In Ohanavan village and its surroundings there are remnants of cyclopean construction (III–I millennium BC) and administrative structures of the congregation (XVII–XVIII).

Saghmosavank

The main church of St. Zion was built in 1215 by the prince Vache Vachutyan. It is a cruciform domed church with two–floor lateral altars in all corners of the building.

The atrium was built in the second half of the XIII century.

Its western entrance has rich decorations.

The atrium is simultaneously connected with both churches, St. Zion and Surb Astvatsatsin (Holy Mother of God) of 1235. In the eastern apse of the church a bas–relief of sun with its rays is carved. Next to the sun in an arch an angel and an eagle holding a ram in his talons are depicted.

The architect also used a combination of various colors, red and black stones, as well as stones painted in white and yellow. There are remnants of frescos preserved in the main apse.

Northeast of the altar there is a library built in 1255, that nowadays serves as a sacristy.

The monastery is located on the edge of the gorge of the river Kasakh with the most picturesque scenery. Northeast of the complex one may see the mountain Arailer (2577 m).

Tympanum of St. Karapet church, Hovhannavank

Aruch

In the V century the village of Aruch was mentioned as the winter camp for royal troops. The nakharar (Armenian prince) Gregory Mamikonyan (661–682) transformed it into his residence. Aruch cathedral (St. Gregory church), one of the most religious and architecturally notable monuments, was also built by Mamikonyan in the 60s of the VII century. It is a hall with a rectangular dome (the latter was not preserved) that amazes with its size (17.0 x 34.6m). The remnants of frescos that present the scene of Ascension can be seen on the interior walls. On the main apse there is a fresco of Jesus Christ (only part of the picture has survived) with a parchment in his left hand. The fresco is 7m in size.

The palace, that was constructed by Gregory Mamikonyan and is located northeast of the cathedral, was discovered during 1948–1951. In Aruch one can still find remnants of mausoleums from the Bronze Age, remains of a fortress, caravanserai (XIII century) etc.

Dashtadem

One of the most interesting historical monuments of Armenia, Dashtadem fortress, founded in the X century during the Bagratid dynasty, is situated on the way to Gyumri, not far from the ruins of Talin Caravansaray (5.5 km from Talin). The last ruler of Ani from the Shadadid (Shadyanid or Shadadyan) dynasty added defensive towers to the citadel in the XII century; an inscription in the Arabic language mentioning the construction can be found at the entrance to the citadel. The construction was continued by the Zakarian princes in the XIII century. The fortress which was located in the northern part of the Silk Road fulfilled defensive role for the city of Ani which was the capital and trade-economic center of that time. There is a notable inscription in the Armenian language at the western entrance to the fortress which dates back to the XIV century. It belongs to Agbug, Ivane Zakarian's son, and tells about a festivity dedicated to the exemption of Talin from the tax on wine. The fortress maintained its strategic value up until the XVIII-XIX centuries. The latest excavations were realized in 2015.

Caravansaray of Aruch, XIII c.

St. Katoghike
of Talin

Talin St. Katoghike cathedral is a domed basilica supposedly from the VII century. It was built by princes of the Kamsarakan family.

Being a triple–nave basilica, thanks to the round shape of the southern and northern apses, it acquires a cross shape from both inside and outside. The quantity of light that enters into the cathedral through 12 windows of the tambour of the dome, 29 windows of the façade and 9 circular windows is absolutely stunning.

The reliefs, carved in stone, are partially polychrome, the combination of black and red tufa, and the remnants of the frescos of Holy Virgin on the principal apse form modest decoration of this luxurious construction.

The cathedral was damaged by the earthquake of 1840 losing part of its dome. In 1947 the cathedral was restored.

Oshakan

In the center of Oshakan the church of St. Mesrop Mashtots built in 1875–79 is situated. It replaced a more ancient one built by Vahan Amatuni in 443. Mashtots' grave is in the crypt of the church. In 1960s the interior of the church got covered with frescos (H. Minasyan). The bell tower of 1884 stands in the east. In the beginning of the XX century during the

Armenian Genocide in Turkey the school, which was on the territory of the church, received and gave shelter to numerous orphans and afterwards served as an orphanage.

Armenian schools have a very interesting tradition of taking the pupils to Mesrop Mashtots' grave, so that they solemnly take an oath and only afterwards start learning the alphabet.

Mastara

Mastara is situated 6km away from the city of Talin. Here one of the most ancient and perfect constructions of medieval Armenia can be found. It comes from the VI-VII centuries. The church was restored in the XIX century. This is a cruciform church with a perfect octahedron dome of 11.2m diameters. There is a window on each side of the tambour. The passage from the cruciform plan into the tambour is very interesting. The angles on the sides are cut in a shape of triangular niches. Gregory the Illuminator had brought the relics of John the Baptist that are now buried next to the church. From this comes the name of the church, which in Armenian means "mas"–piece, "tara"–I took.

Ararat region

Distance:	29km southwest from Yerevan to Artashat
Centre:	Artashat (26 thousand inhabitants)
Number of cities:	4
	(Artashat, Ararat, Masis, Vedi)
Number of villages:	95
Population:	280 thousand inhabitants
Altitude:	1600–2300m
Monasteries and churches:	Khor Virap, Hovhannes-Karapet, Stepanos
Fortresses:	Kaqavaberd
Citadels:	Artashat, Dvin
Other places of interest:	Vishapakars (dragon stones), Khosrov National Park

Ararat region borders Turkey in the west, Azerbaijan (Nakhijevan) in the Southwest, Armavir region in the Northwest, Kotayk in the Northeast, Gegharkunik in the East and Vayots Dzor in the Southeast. The climate of the region is dry. The mountainous area of the region is composed of rocks and mountains of Urtsi and Yeranos.

Hovhannes–Karapet

According to the inscriptions, the Spitakavor church of Surb Astvatsatsin (Holy Mother of God) of Hovhannes–Karapet monastery was built in 1301. The only western entrance is decorated with magnificent bas-reliefs. Southwest of the church there is a XIV century chapel currently standing in ruins, which is attached to a two–floor mausoleum located west of the church (the rotunda of the bell–tower is destroyed).

*Persian leopard,
Khosrov National Park*

Khosrov National Park

Khosrov National Park, which occupies 27000 ha, is also situated in Ararat region. Founded by king Khosrov in the III century, it has been a National Park since 1958. On the low slopes of the mountain the landscape is semi–dry.

The forest vegetation has been extended up to the medium altitude in the form of oak and juniper forests. Spindle, sorbus, and Caucasian honeysuckle can also be found there. It is typical to see mouflon and wild goat in the local fauna. One may also see leopard, lynx, pine marten, wolf, fox, badger, wild boar and brown bear.

In the mountainous part of the region there is almost no population; the plain is inhabited.

Artashat

In 176 B.C. king Artashes I founded a city in the Ararat valley giving it his name. Plutarch and Strabo considered that Hannibal was directly involved in the construction of Artashat. Plutarch wrote - "It is known that Carthaginian general Hannibal moved to the court of Artashes I and gave him pieces of useful advice after Antioch completely lost the war against the Romans".

Artashat was situated on the slopes of Mount Ararat, on the left bank of the river Araxes in the area adjacent to the mouth of the river Metsamor. The citadel and the central quarters were situated on nine hills, on one of which Khor Virab monastery is currently situated. By the way, a more ancient fortress belonging to the Urartian period was located in the same place. The geographical location of Artashat was very beneficial-this area of Ararat valley was a crossroad of important commercial routes going from south to north and from east to west. Immediately after the construction it gained a huge economic significance, became one of the most important transit centers of international trade (including the Silk Road), as a result of which Armenian merchants started to import raw silk from China (cocoons or primary commodities) and silk fabrics, and exported copper, lead, gold embroidered fabric, glasswork and vessels from Alexandria and Mesopotamia.

The outskirts of the city were surrounded by a wall approximately 10 km long and were connected to each other by means of narrow corridors in between the hills. According to J. D. Khachatryan (who was the leader of archeological expedition exploring the site in 1970s and the author of the book "Artashat, Antique Necropolis") one of the prominent researchers on Artashat, the territory of the city of Artashat was 400 ha, the length of the fortification-10 000 meters, the population of the city was 150 000. As the result of archeological excavations the ruins of ancient temple dedicated to Tir were found. It used to be a magnificent construction as illustrated by the ruins of fine pillars decorated with carvings, in some places resembling the ones in Garni. On the territory adjacent to the temple a public bath was found. The public bath gives entirely new concept of the development level of domestic culture in Armenia in those distant days, the preserved fragments of the mosaic strike with their remarkable beauty. The archeological expedition of NAS RA has been excavating the territory of historical Artashat for a long period of time.

Khor Virap

Khor Virap fortress monastery is located on the hill close to Poqr Vedi village. During the ancient times the historical city of Artashat, as well as Khor Virap citadel were located here. There was a prison of the courtyard in the place of the current monastery. It was in one of its dungeons that Gregory the Illuminator spent 13 years. In 642 Catholicos Nerses III ordered to construct a chapel on top of the saint dungeon.

In its structure the chapel has some similarities to Zvartnots temple. In 1662 a basilica was built where the chapel used to stand. On the right side of the main altar there is a dungeon with metallic stairs, which enables thousands of pilgrims that visit the monastery, to climb up and down easily. The dungeon has 6.5m in depth and 4.4m in diameters.

Northeast of St Gregory church Surb Astvatsatsin church (Holy Mother of God) of the XVII century with a bell tower is situated.

Within the walls that surround the two churches there are several auxiliary constructions: refectory, cells etc. The name Khor Virap originates from Armenian words "khor" — deep and "virap" — citadel.

Kaqavaberd

The fortress was built on the right bank of the Azat river. Since IX–X centuries it was mentioned as a property of Bagratid dynasty. Afterwards it was transferred to Pahlavuni and later on to Proshyan family. The fortress lived through lots of invasions. Nevertheless it is well preserved nowadays. As it is located on the slope of a mountain, there is no access from its three sides. Its northeastern walls have 2–2.5m width with towers of 8–10m height. Within the fortress the church and other constructions have been preserved.

Dvin

It was decided to move the capital city of the Armenian state to a different place immediately after the riverbed of the Araxes changed towards the south and the capital city Artashat was left without water supply. The king of Great Armenia Khosrov II from Arsacid dynasty chose the hill of Dvin for this purpose. The king built here his palace in 335 and from that period of time the residence of the Armenian Arsacid royal dynasty, as well as the residence of the head of the Armenian Church were located here. The city was located on a hill, on the top of which there was an old Citadel and adjacent buildings. There were defensive walls composed of two sectors and a tower.

The city grew fast having more than 100 000 inhabitants. Dvin was considered to be one of the most densely populated and the richest cities east from Constantinople. The goods produced in those countries were imported to Dvin. The goods of the artists from Dvin were exported far beyond the country's borders: glasswork, earthenware, ceramics, weapons as well as rugs. The city had its own customs. Dvin very soon became the economic center of the region, a meeting point for commercial routes joining the east to the west. Six trade routes started from Dvin which connected the city with Persian cities, Bagdad, Byzantine Empire and with Mediterranean countries. At the end of the VII century as a result of Arab invasion the city, as well as a greater part of the country were controlled by the Arab Caliphate. The Arabs formed an administrative unit of Armenia with Dvin as its central city. Written foreign and local sources call Dvin "Great capital". Though the territory of Dvin served as the battlefield between the Arabs and the Byzantine Empire in the next 2 centuries, in the IX century it was still a developing city. In 1236 Dvin was conquered by the Mongols. Though it was robbed and destroyed it managed to survive another century. Several small villages that have survived up until now were constructed in the place of the city.

Residence of the Catholicos

Armavir region

Distance:	20km west from Yerevan to Vagharshapat
Centre:	Armavir (33 thousand inhabitants)
Number of cities:	3
	(Vagharshapat, Armavir, Metsamor)
Number of villages:	95
Population:	285 thousand inhabitants
Monasteries and churches:	*Ejmiadzin, Gayane, Hripsime, Zvartnots, Shogakat, S. Astvatsatsin*
Other places of interest:	*the ruins of the Urartian city Argishtikhinili, those of the ancient capital Yervandashat, Sardarapat monument*

In the South and Southwest Armavir region borders Turkey, in the North Aragatsotn region, in the East Yerevan and in the Southeast Ararat region. The climate of the region is dry. The only river that starts in the region is Metsamor. The only nuclear power plant of both the country and the whole region is situated here.

The region is rich with peculiar historical monuments. A Bronze Age foundry (5000 years) on the slope of the river Metsamor is of special interest. The ruins of the Urartian city of Argishtikhinili carry an immense historical value. Nearby, on the left bank of the old riverbed of Araks, the ancient capital of Armenia, Armavir is situated. More to the west, in the delta of the Araks and Akhuryan rivers, there are ruins of another ancient capital, Yervandashat.

The Metsamor Museum

In the ancient settlement of Metsamor a citadel, a unique temple complex, an ancient copper-bronze metallurgical complex (III mil B.C.) which covered the whole cycle of metal processing, an observatory for watching the celestial bodies, residential constructions with round basis built in the early Bronze Age made with raw brick, urban settlements dating back to the Late Bronze Age and a huge burial complex were found during the archeological excavations which lasted more than 50 years.

For thousands of years the settlement of Metsamor was the trade, industrial, scientific and religious center of the entire Ancient East, in particular for the Armenian highland. The museum has 28 000 artifacts which date back from the Chalcolithic Age (V-IV mil. B.C.) to the Late Middle Ages (17-18 c.). Unique exhibits are displayed in the museum among which are the oldest gold jewelry found in Armenia, a unique agate frog used as a weight, an Egyptian cornelian seal with Babylonian inscription and Egyptian hieroglyphs. The museum displays a reorganization of a burial place typical of the Late Bronze Age.

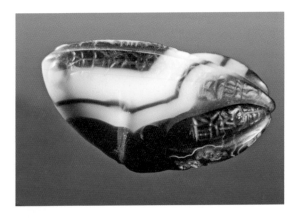
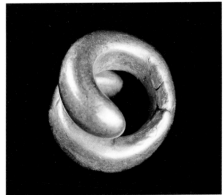

Sardarapat

Sardarapat monument presents a great historical and architectural value. Being built in 1968 by the architect Israyeylan, it symbolizes the great victory of the Armenian nation in 1918 against the Ottoman Turkey. The arcades with bells that rise to the sky remind the bells that were ceaselessly ringing during those seven days of the fight. From both sides there are bulls with wings in front of the bells impeding the entrance of the enemy. 100m away from the monument there is an ethnographic museum.

The main reason for the construction of the State "Sardarapat" Ethnographic Museum was preserving the material which referred to May battles. The central hall is dedicated to those events, as well as the history of the formation of the first Republic of Armenia. The museum also exhibits artifacts of material culture of Armenia of different periods, starting from the Bronze Age to national costumes and rugs of the 20th century.

Ejmiadzin

It is situated 21km west of Yerevan, in the center of Vagharshapat city. According to the tradition, during 60 days of preaching Gregory the Illuminator had a dream that Jesus descended from the sky with a golden hammer and revealed to him a place, where he was to construct the first Armenian Christian church instead of a pagan temple. Gregory followed God's will and named the place Ejmiadzin according to the Armenian meaning "ej" descent and "miadzin" the only begotten. According to the testimonies of historian Agathangeghos, the cathedral was built close to the royal palace during the first years of Christianity in Armenia (301–303).

Remnants of a pre–Christian construction were discovered underneath the current building. The cathedral acquired its actual cruciform composition in 483 during the reconstruction implemented by Vahan Mamikonyan (except the dome).

■ *Spear of Longinus*

The actual dome is the result of a reconstruction in the XVII century. Persian shah Abas, after exiling the Armenians to Persia, wanted to completely destroy the cathedral and transport its stones to Persia in order to build a new one there, in this manner making Armenians get attached to the new land. However, it was decided that only "considerable" stones would be transferred; those were taken out and moved to Jolfa. This was the core reason of further deterioration of the ramshackle Cathedral.

In 1629-1632 reconstruction work was carried out. The dome, roof, ceiling and foundation were restored. In 1658 new walls and refectory, bell tower and other parts of the building were constructed. Hovnatanyan restored the frescos of the Cathedral in the XVIII century. In 1869 by the initiative of Catholicos Gevorg IV a museum was attached to the eastern part of the Cathedral. In 1955 Catholicos Vazgen I also implemented some restoration work.

A seminary, residence of the Catholicos of All Armenians, St John Baptist church, administrative buildings, khachkars (cross stones), among which is one of the most ancient Savour's khachkar (IX century), are located on the territory of the Cathedral. There are also several buildings under construction in the area of Ejmiadzin.

Hripsime

St. Hripsime church (please have a look at the history of the Virgin in "Religion" section) was built in 618 by the Catholicos Komitas and is 500m east of Ejmiadzin cathedral. According to the tradition a chapel was constructed on top of Gregory the Illuminator's tomb previously destroyed by Persians.

Walls were built around the church in 1776, as well as lateral windows of the altar apse were set. In 1880 a two-tier bell-tower with an eight-column belfry was added to it. External niches were used for the first time in St. Hripsime church.

The church belongs to the most perfect type of religious constructions of the medieval Armenia. It is a cruciform temple with a centered dome, where the architecture splendidly highlights the integrity of the interior space. Despite its small size, the church looks majestic.

Zvartnots

St. Gregory temple of Zvartnots is situated 3km south of Vagharshapat city. The name translated from the archaic Armenian sounds like "celestial angels".

According to historians the construction of the cathedral commenced in 642 under the guidance of Catholicos Nerses (the Constructor) who built a majestic cathedral dedicated to St. Gregory, where supposedly the meeting of Gregory the Illuminator and Tiridates III took place. After the Arab occupation of Dvin Nerses transferred the patriarch palace of Catholicos from Dvin to Vagharshapat. Zvartnots survived until the X century. Historical sources provide no data about the cause of its fall. Its remnants were discovered in the beginning of the XX century.

The excavations additionally revealed that Zvartnots stands out among the rest of the structures that date back to Urartian kingdom of Rusa II. The majority of scholars approve the reconstruction of 1905 by Toros Toromanian, who worked during the original excavations. According to the original project, the temple had three floors.

The interior of the church, decorated with mosaics, had a shape of a Greek cross with a passage surrounding this area, while the external one was a polygon of 32 sides. Nowadays, the first floor is partially reconstructed (with 35.75m in diameter). The façades of the temple are decorated with bas-reliefs representing pomegranates, grapes, grape leaves, eagles, the architects and the workers of the temple. Sainte–Chapelle of Paris has a relief picturing Zvartnots on mountain Ararat. Together with Ejmiadzin, Zvartnots cathedral was added to the UNESCO World Heritage list in 2000.

Gayane

St. Gayane church (situated 200m south of Ejmiadzin Cathedral) was built by the Catholicos Ezr in 630 on top of Virgin Gayane's tomb (please have a look at the history of the Virgin in "Religion" section).

According to its architectural composition, it is a triple–nave domed basilica. In 1652 it was restored and during the same period a gallery was added in the western part.

Gegharkunik region

Distance:	92km northeast from Yerevan to Gavar
Centre:	Gavar (26 thousand inhabitants)
Population:	242 thousand inhabitants
Number of cities:	5
	(Gavar, Sevan Tchambarak, Martuni, Vardenis)
Number of villages:	93
The highest mountains:	Azhdahak (3598m), Spitakasar (3555m), Vardenis (3522m), Geghasar (3446m)
Monasteries and churches:	*Sevanavank, Hayravank, Hatsarat, Gavar, Vanevan*
Other places of interest:	*Noratus*
Landscape:	*Geghama mountain range, Artanish, Lake Sevan*

Gegharkunik borders Tavush and Lori regions in the North, Vayots Dzor in the South, Ararat region in the Southwest, Kotayk in the West and Azerbaijan in the East.

Lake Sevan

Lake Sevan

Lake Sevan occupies ¼ of the territory of the region. Its primary inflows are 28 rivers and streams. 10% of the outgoing water is drained by the river Hrazdan. Along with Lake Van and Lake Urmia, Sevan was considered one of the three great lakes of the historical Armenian Kingdom and it is the only one left within the boundaries of the modern Republic of Armenia. The name Sevan in Armenian literally means "Black Van" being compared to Lake Van.

Before human intervention dramatically changed the eco–system, the lake had 95m in depth covering an area of 1360km². In 1933 the Armenian Supreme Soviet started implementing a plan of reducing the water level by 55meters and using the water for irrigation and obtaining hydroelectricity. Walnut trees and oaks were planted on newly acquired land; introduction of some trout species into the remainder of the lake increased fishery production tenfold. An ecological disaster like the one in Aral Sea was avoided when the Stalinist era ended

in 1953 and the project with all its consequences was thoroughly reviewed. As there were difficulties with planting oaks and walnut trees, as well as with fishery, the Sevan Committee was established with a mission «to raise the level for as much as possible». Hydroelectric power stations located on Hrazdan were replaced with thermal power stations.

Nowadays the lake has a surface of 1240km². Sevan trout (Salmo ischchan) is an endemic fish species of Lake Sevan comprising 30% of the fish of the lake. However, it was endangered because of the introduction of various competitors, such as common whitefish, goldfish and crayfish from the Danube river.

Archaeological excavations done in the drained area of the lake enabled the scientists to discover that 3500 years ago the major part of the Lake was dry. Cyclopean constructions (Lchashen, Hayravank), mausoleums, building and inscriptions from the Urartian period were discovered.

Sevanavank

Sevanavank monastery, situated on Sevan peninsula (before an island), was founded by Gregory the Illuminator in 305. During the Bronze Age the island was fortified with a wall; there was a pagan temple then. The current monastery was built in 874 by the king Ashot I, the founder of the Bagratid dynasty, and his daughter Mariam. Two churches, St. Arakelots and St. Astvatsatsin are still there.

According to the historians of the era, the monastery of the island was mainly used for pilgrimage and worship, as well as a refuge for noble Armenians, who fell into disgrace. It was also the headquarters of king Ashot I since the time he started a fight against Arab invaders in 859. The monastery continued its activity up to the XX century, until the last monk

left it in 1930. The monastery nowadays is supported and maintained by the church, which uses the monastery as a summer pension for the seminarians. There are two churches that have reached our days; Surb Arakelots (St. Apostles) and Surb Astvatsatsin (Holy Mother of God). West of the first church there are ruins of one of the most ancient atriums of Armenia used up to 1930. On top of the hill there are ruins of the third church.

Noratus

On the right bank of the river Gavaraget, 5km northeast of Gavar Noratus village is situated. In the southern part of the village there is a cemetery with its numerous khachkars (cross stones). The majority of them are from the X-XVII centuries. Some are installed in groups, forming a family mausoleum. There is a vast amount of solitary khachars as well.

Hayravank

In Hayravank monastery, constructed during the IX–XII centuries on the shore of Lake Sevan, a church from the IX century and an atrium (gavit) from the XII century, which belongs to a two–column atrium type, have survived. Architectural spirit of this church presents a rough draft of the XIII century masterpiece. One may grasp the aspiration of finding a new style with its characteristic features, though they are still far from perfection.

Tsaghkadzor

Kotayk region

Distance:	50km northeast from Yerevan to Hrazdan
Centre:	Hrazdan (54 thousand inhabitants)
Population:	282 thousand inhabitants
Number of cities:	7
	(Abovyan, Hrazdan, Charentsavan, Byureghavan, Tsaghkadzor, Nor Hatchn, Yeghvard)
The highest mountain:	Arailer (2577m)
Monasteries and churches:	*Geghard, Kecharis, Getargel, Yeghvard, Zoravar, Bjni, Teghenyats, Maqravan, Neghuts, Ptghni, Mayravank*
Fortresses:	*Garni, Arinj*
Landscape:	*Arailer, Artanish, Garni gorge, Geghama Mountains, Hatis*

Kotayk is the only region that does not have external state borders. It borders the capital in the Southwest, Aragatsotn region in the West, Tavush region in the Northeast, Lori region in

the North, Gegharkunik in the East and Ararat in the South. The health resorts of Arzni and Hanqavan, being next to the springs, are situated in Kotayk region.

Tsaghkadzor ski resort

Tsaghkadzor is situated 55km northeast away from Yerevan. It is a resort with Olympic Sport Council and excellent ski slopes. Tsaghkadzor ropeway was established not so long ago (2008). It is divided into 4 stations; the first one has 1137m in length, the second is 1458m, the third 1624m and the fourth 926m long. Shifting from one lift to another can be easily done without taking off the equipments. The snowboarders and the skiers also have drag lifts at their disposal. The ropeway is constructed in Teghenis mountains. Tsaghkadzor is a resort completely prepared both for summer and winter tourism. The winter here is mild but snowy with 270 sunny days per year. As a result of heavy snowing the snow cover is around 1.4m thick. The gorges of Hrazdan and Azat rivers are natural masterpieces. The geographic formations, generated as a result of lava activity, are highly impressive.

Geghard monastery

Geghard monastery is located 35km northeast of Yerevan.

The monastery of Geghard is a unique architectural construction partially carved out of the adjacent mountain and surrounded by cliffs. It is listed as the UNESCO World Heritage List. The monastic complex, founded in the IV century, was originally called Ayrivank meaning "the Monastery of the Cave". The name commonly used for the monastery today is Geghardavank, means "the Monastery of the Spear" and is due to the spear that had been brought to Armenia by the Apostle Thaddeus. Nothing has survived from Ayrivank structures.

The main church was built in 1215 under the auspices of Zakare and Ivane Zakaryan brothers. The second phase of the construction of the monastery began with the acquisition of the cathedral by the prince Proshyan in the second half of the XIII century. During a short period of time Proshyan constructed cavernous structures. A series of both architectonic and artistic works were excavated in the north on different levels of rock adjacent to the main church; below two smaller churches, an atrium, as well as an enormous mausoleum atrium with four columns were found. The first one located northwest of the atrium was excavated in 1230–1250. One may notice an inscription with the architect' name on the dome: Galdzak. In 1283 the second church and atrium were excavated; it is supposed to be the mausoleum of Proshyan family. On the northern wall of the atrium there is a medium relief representing an ox–head and two caged lions. Below there is an eagle holding a ram in its talons.

West of the atrium stairs lead to the mausoleum of Papak Proshyan (1288). There are many ornaments and reliefs both inside the church, as well as on its façades. There are also a lot of khachkars (cross stones) and cells carved in the rock around the church. Geghard monastery presents an enormous value for the Armenian culture and architecture.

Geghard monastery

Garni temple

Garni fortress is situated less than 30km northeast of Yerevan (before reaching Geghard).The fortress stands on a triangular cape surrounded by deep cliffs. Archeological excavations of the area and its remnants allow the historians to claim that the fortress dates back to the III century BC.

Back then it was a summer residence of two Armenian royal dynasties: Artaxid and Arsacid. During the first half of the I century it was destroyed by the Romans. According to the Greek inscription, which can be seen on the main entrance of the fortress, king Tiridates I restored it in the same century. The latter built the temple dedicated to God Mihr (Mithra).

The fortress was protected with walls from the north.

The length of the walls is 374m and they have 14 towers. The 24-column Greco–Roman style temple stands in the center of the fortress. East of the temple there are remnants of the circular church from the VII century. Below, almost on the edge of the canyon, one may find ruins of the royal palace. Next to the temple excavators discovered the ruins of a bath–house (dating back to the I century). This Roman style construction consists of separate rooms with hot, warm and cold water. It includes a complicated system of making the circular air hot from the bottom of the ground. Wonderful multicolor mosaics with images of fish, Gods and other mythological creatures decorate its floor. The temple of Garni was destroyed and reconstructed several times; Arabs, Mongols, and Turks repeatedly crossed this area. Garni even experienced an earthquake in 1679, resulting in the whole complex getting buried in ashes. It was only in the 1950s that excavations and reconstructions of the temple were launched (architecture Shahinyan).

Havuts Tar

Havuts Tar is situated east of Garni on top of the mountain on the left bank of the river Azat. This monastic complex is divided into two types of constructions. The main church of the western group (XIII) was built with a combination of various colorful stones (is in ruins). The main church Amenaprkich (the Savour) of the eastern group was built during the X–XI centuries and was reconstructed in the XIII century.
In 1679 it was destroyed by an earthquake. St. Karapet church was built during the reconstruction of the XVIII century.

Kecharis

The monastery is situated in the city of Tsaghkadzor. In accordance with the inscription of the southern wall, the main church of St.Gregory the Illuminator was built in 1003 by Gregory Magistros. It is a domed hall with 10.4m in diameter. The rectangular atrium with four columns is in the south (XII century).
South of the main building there are churches of Surb Nshan (Saint Sign) of the XI century and Katoghike of the XIII century. The latter is the most luxurious in the complex. St. Harutyun (Resurrection) church is located 120m south of the main complex.

Vayots Dzor region

Distance:	123km southeast from Yerevan to Yeghegnadzor
Centre:	Yeghegnadzor (8 thousand inhabitants)
Population:	56 thousand inhabitants
The number of cities:	3
	(Yeghegnadzor, Vayk, Jermuk)
The number of villages:	52
Monasteries and churches:	*Noravank, Gladzor, Gndevank, Yeghegis, Zorats, Tanade, Areni, Arkazi, Spitakavor, Tsaghats Qar*
Fortresses:	*Smbatavan, Proshaberd*
Other places of interest:	*Selim Caravanserai, Magil and Mozrov cave*
Landscape:	*Jermuk waterfall, Arpa river valley*

Wine festival, Areni village

Vayots Dzor region borders Nakhijevan (Azerbaijan) in the West, Syunik in the Southeast, Karabakh in the East and Ararat in the North. Vayots Dzor region is a region of mountains and rocks. Mountain slopes are torn everywhere by deep gorges and cliffs. The principal road of the region goes through difficult passes and gorges of high mountains. Its highest pass Selim (2410m) connects the region with Gegharkunik.

The caves are typical elements of Vayots Dzor region and among them the most famous ones are Magil and Mozrov caves. The latter was discovered during the road construction. It has more than 300m in depth. Within the cave in its enormous "rooms" one may see a huge amount of stalactites and stalagmites all the way from the bottom to the top.

Areni 1 – Birds' Cave

Layers of the remnants of cultural materials dating to different periods of Chalcolithic Age were discovered in some of the halls of the cave as well at the slope near the entrance during the archeological excavations in 2007-2008. However, it was the finding of the oldest leather shoe on earth which is 5500 years old that shook the whole scientific world (according to the research done by NAS RA and Oxford University laboratories; it is currently displayed at the National History Museum).

Well-preserved vessels used for food storage, jugs as well as wine press found in the cave indicate that the complex had economic importance. This is also proved by well-preserved remnants of grapes, apricots, plums, barley, wheat and other wild and cultivated seeds which were found near or inside the vessels. There is also a theory about the cave as a ceremonial center. The results from the carbon-14 data of bones, carbon, seeds and other organic remnants suggest that these layers date back to the last quarter of the V millennium B.C. and the first half of the IV millennium B.C.

Areni 1 is one of the most unique and well-preserved monuments of Late Chalcolithic Age which not only provides possibilities to investigate the peculiarities of material culture of V-IV millennium B.C., but also confirms 6000- year-old Armenian wine making tradition.

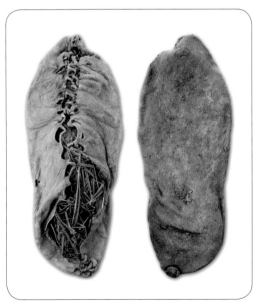 

Areni-1 cave and the oldest shoe

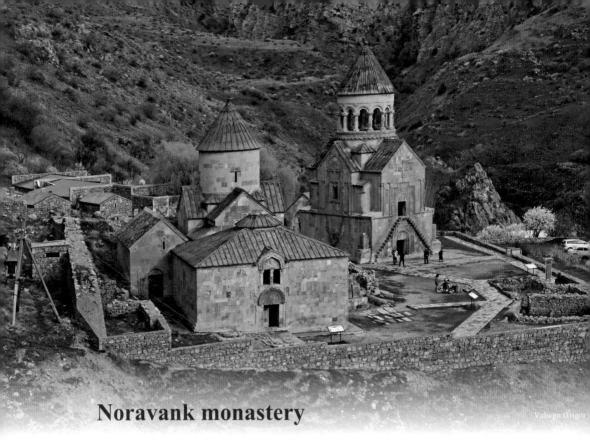

Noravank monastery

Vahagn Grigor

The monastery is situated 3km northeast of Amaghu village at the very end of an amazing rocky gorge. It has been a sacred place since the early Middle Ages. However, the construction of the current complex dates back to the XIII–XIV centuries, with an exception of the ruins of St. Karapet (St. John the Precursor) dating back to the IX century. It is located south of St. Stephan church. XIV century two-story St. Astvatsatsin church (Holy Mother of God) is in the center of the complex. It was constructed upon the request of prince Burtel Orbelyan. For this reason it is sometimes called Burtelashen. The first floor, which is semi–excavated in the ground, is the mausoleum of the prince. The narrow console stone stairs, projecting from the façade, lead to the second floor. One may get amazed at the quantity of the reliefs on the façades. The lintels of both floors are worth mentioning; on the lintel of the second floor the image of Christ, figures of Apostles Peter and Paul are carved and on that of the first floor the images of the Holy Virgin with Archangels Gabriel and Michael at her sides can be seen. The church is crowned with a 12-column dome. On some of the preserved original columns there are reliefs of Holy Virgin, prince Orbelyan and his son. Two well–known architects of medieval Armenia worked on the construction of the monastery: Siranes in the second half of the XIII and an architect, miniaturist and sculptor Momik in the XIV century. The principal unit of the complex, St.Stepanos (St.Stephen, 1216–1223) church, is located northwest of St.Astvatsatsin church. The atrium (gavit) is in the western part and was built in the XIII century. In the XIV century it was most probably reconstructed by Momik. Except its original architectural composition, this building also surprises with the image of God the Father cut on the tympanum, which was an unprecedented phenomenon in the medieval Armenian and demonstrates the artists' liberty of thought in expressing the Biblical canonic themes. Along the northern wall of St.Stepanos church one may notice a hidden mausoleum church of St. Gregory (1275), where the members of Orbelyan family were buried. Under one of the gravestone, with a stretching lion over it, was the prince Elicum Orbelyan. The monastery was fortified with walls during the XVII–XVIII centuries. Around the monastery, adjacent to the walls, there are ruins of administrative and economic constructions. Because of the earthquake of 1931 the monastery was highly damaged and it was only in 1998 that the reconstruction work was carried out thanks to the support of the Canadian– Armenian benefactor Hatchetyan.

Noravank ravine

Gladzor University

Gladzor University is situated close to Vernashen village. It was an extremely important center of education of the medieval Armenia. It was first mentioned as a university in 1291, founded in Tanade monastery by the initiative of the prince Prosh Khaghbakyan and with the support of Orbelyan princes. Theology, philosophy, music, grammar, logic, arithmetic, astrology, geometry and other sciences were taught at this University. In order to be able to study at this university people from various regions of Armenia and Cilicia were coming here. The studies lasted for 7–8 years. The graduates were receiving the title of "Archimandrite" and were allowed to teach afterwards.

Smbataberd fortress

Smbataberd fortress is located east of Artabuynk village.

The preserved references dating back to the V century tell a story of a battle between Armenians and Persians close to the fortress.

It has wide and high basalt walls (2–3m). The fortress is protected by deep gorges of Artabuynk and Yeghegis. Remnants of a castle, houses and water deposits are still here. The fortress was restored in 2006–2007.

Jermuk

Jermuk city plays a special role in the region, as well as in the country. It is highly famous for its hot springs and mineral water. It is believed that local water has curative, healing power and has been used to treat a number of digestive problems. The city is located 2000-2080m high above sea level. The predominance of sunny days, healing waters, mild climate, divine nature and other conditions contribute to the fact that Jermuk has always been a first-class resort area. A huge number of modern high-quality hotels (with treatment procedures) and guest houses will ensure your wonderful rest and effective treatment.

Zorats St. Astvatsatsin Church

Zorats church is located in Yeghegis village. In was built before 1303 by the architect Momik and was dedicated to military service. Before leaving for a battle warriors used to enter the church on their horses to get a blessing.

Its extraordinary structure is a wonderful illustration of this. The church does not have a hall. It consists of one–meter high altar and three triangular niches above it, as well as two lateral altars. There is an open area in front of the altar.

The existence of such churches is the proof of the power of Orbelyan princes, who were maintaining a big army.

Selim Caravanserai

Selim Caravanserai is situated in the mountain pass at a height of 2300m. Built in 1332 by the request of prince Chesar Orbelyan, it substituted an ancient caravanserai of the IV century. As all caravanserais, it was located on the commercial route (later called as a silk road) built as a passage for camels (approx. 30 km).

It served as a shelter for medieval traders. The building is a hall made of three basalt naves (13 x 26 m) with a roof. The entrance is made of stalactite with reliefs representing a bull and a lion with a human face and a crown. Water was supplied directly into the hall. East of the hall ruins of a storage were preserved. It was reconstructed in the 1950s.

Khustup Mountain, Kapan

Syunik region

Distance:	320km south from Yerevan to Kapan
Centre:	Kapan (45.5 thousand inhabitants)
Population:	153 thousand inhabitants
The number of cities:	7
	(Kapan, Kajaran, Goris, Sisian, Meghri, Agarak, Dastakert)
The number of villages:	127
The highest mountain:	Kaputjugh (3905m)
Monasteries and churches:	*Tatev, Vorotnavank, Vahanavank, Sisavan*
Fortresses:	*Vorotnaberd, Halidzor*
Other places of interest:	*Zorats Karer (Karahunj) observatory, Devil's bridge, Tatev desert, Akhitu, Khndzoresk village*
Landscape:	*Vorotan river, Shaki waterfall*

Syunik borders reach Vayots Dzor region in the North, Iran in the South, Nakhijevan (Azerbaijan) in the West and Nagorno Karabakh in the East. Syunik is the most mountainous region of the country. The difference between the highest point (Kaputjugh 3905m) and the lowest one (Meghri gorge–375m) is 3500m.

The biggest river is Vorotan and it is known for its gorge,which has 800m depth. Here the river flows under the "Devil's" natural bridge. Shaki waterfall, that has 18m height, was formed in the tributary of the river Vorotan.

Relics Park of plane trees

The biggest relics park of natural plane trees in the world is located south of Kapan city in the gorge of the river Tsav. It occupies the area of 120 ha. The height of some trees of this park reaches 30–35m with 3m in diameter.

Goris

Goris, quite rightly considered to be one of the nicest cities in the country, is located in Syunik region. After 1931 earthquake the city was moved more to the East. In pursuit of constructing new houses for the population, equal parcels of land were distributed and certain norms of structure established.

Thanks to this initiative the old part of the town is full of houses built similarly on the same line. However, at night the city does not have proper lighting and it is better to enjoy its charm during the day.

Khndzoresk

8km from Goris, 1580m above sea level between the gorges and cliffs in the heart of extraordinary nature the old village of Khndzoresk is situated. The village has been abandoned for 50–60 years.

People, who used to live here, mostly built their houses in caves.

Some of them were on 20–30m in height, whereas the ceiling of one "apartment" was the ground of the other one. In 1913 Khndzoresk had 1800 inhabitants and 7 schools.

Later inhabitants were moved to the plain, which is less than 1km away from the old village. Nowadays, only the tourists visit the old village. Their number increased after the construction of the famous "hanging" bridge, that unites two sides of the ravine (2012). The tomb of Mkhitar Sparapet, the commander of the Armenian troops (XVIII), can be found here.

Tatev

Tatev monastery founded in the IV century was an extremely important center of education. The monastery was being built in succession during the IX–X and XVII–XVIII centuries. The most ancient construction that has survived up to now is St. Paul and St. Peter cathedral, which came to replace the one ruined in 895–906. The cathedral was built by the initiative of bishop Hovhannes and the support of prince Ashot and his wife Shushan. It is a spacious rectangular hall with lateral altars. The cylindrical dome that crowns the church surprises with its height and shape.

The original dome was destroyed in the course of the earthquake of 1138 and was reconstructed in 1274. In 930 the walls of the cathedral were decorated with frescos; the main apse depicted the Pantocrator, sitting on a throne, surrounded by three prophets and four saints. On the western apse one may see the grand scene of the Final Judgment. Finally, the northern one depicted the Birth. Almost none of them survived.

In the XVIII century, adjacent to the southern apse, a mausoleum of Grigor Tatevatsi was built. At the end of the XIX a bell tower was added in the western side.

St.Astvatsatsin church, which is to the left from the entrance, was built in 1087 forming the second floor of the mausoleum. In 1295 south of the cathedral St. Gregory church was built. In was called to replace the old church of the same saint that was destroyed by an earthquake. It is assumed that the construction was implemented by Momik by the order of the prince Orbelyan. Along with this building an unsteady "baton" (Gavazan) was installed at the center of the yard in the beginning of the X century. It has an octahedral lace bounded with borders allowing it to move despite being a basalt construction rising 6m in height.

Oil Mill, Tatev

There are several versions about that it served as a warning sign The principal unit is surrounded the refectory, bakery, kitchen, located inside the walls, there and a bathhouse outside the invasions and earthquakes many occasions. The devastating the monastery manuscripts to ashes. During burned down. After the last the 1970s. The name Tatev

the objective of this obelisk. Many believe of earthquakes and arrivals of the enemy. by walls. Within those walls one can find library and cells. Besides the buildings are also an oil mill ("dzit han"), a school walls north of the entrance. Various damaged the monastic complex on Seljuk invasion was the cruelest one and burning more than 10 thousand Tamerlan invasion the whole unit was earthquake of 1931 it was reconstructed in means "ta"– give and "tev" –wings.

Wings of Tatev

In order to get to Tatev monastery (approximately 20km northwest of Goris) one may use the "Tatever" ropeway ("Wings of Tatev") inaugurated in 2010, which is the longest in the world, consisting of one section of 5750m. The ropeway was built in the framework of Tatev Revival Project thanks to private financial assistance (businessman Ruben Vardanyan and others). The maximum depth is 380m. The route is completed in 10–12 minutes.

Zorats Karer (Karahunj)

One of the most ancient megalithic monuments of the world is located close to Sisian city. On the plateau of 1770m height above sea level, occupying 7 ha area there are menhirs of 1.5x 2.8m in size weighing 8.5 tons. There are more than 200 stones there. Some of them bear smooth angled spy holes of 4–5 cm in diameter and conical widening at the end. There is also a periscope. Those extended monoliths are located from East to West.

The central ellipse of the monument is comprised of 40 stones standing upright (there are also some laid down on the ground).

There are diverse versions about the meaning of the monument. Nevertheless, the version of academic Heruni is the most investigated one. Some of them bear smooth angled spy holes of 4–5 cm in diameter and conical widening at the end. In September 2010 the University of Oxford together with Royal Geographical Society of Great Britain examined Karahunj and according to the head of the expedition the monument can be one of the most ancient observatories in the world. According to other versions Karahunj could also be a temple of the God Ara or an old university. The name Karahunj is translated as "qar"–stone and "hunj"– song, sound.

Petroglyphs, VII century BC, Mount Ishkhanasar

Vorotnavank

Vorotnavank is located 2km south of Vaghatin village. According to historian S.Orbelyan, St.Gregory church, which is in ruins at the moment, was a single–nave church and was founded by Gregory the Illuminator and known for its magic power to cure the snakebite. The buildings are located alongside the rectangular yard.

The most ancient construction is St. Stepanos (Stephan, 1000) church. In the Southeast St. Karapet church, decorated with frescos, was situated.

Unfortunately, only the remains of the carvings on the northern apse have been preserved. On the western part remains of an atrium and other constructions can be found.

Places of interest in Artsakh

Monasteries and churches:	*Gandzasar, Dadivank, Ghazanchechots, Tsitsernavank, Gtchavank, Lusavorich, Kanach Jam, Nngi, Avetaranots, Shoshka, Azogh, Amaras, Bovurjanavank*
Fortresses:	*Shushi, Tigranakert, Kachaghakaberd, Handaberd, Mayraberd*
Other places of interest:	*Jermajur spring, the plane tree of Skhtorashen*
The highest mountain:	*Gomshasar (3724m)*

The historical name of this region in Armenian is Artsakh. The name of Nagorno Karabakh, which in Russian means mountainous, is absolutely justified taking into account its relief, mountainous sceneries, gorges and the quantity of winding, twisting roads. The nature of Artsakh keeps surprising its visitors. On the bank of the river Tartar, 20 km away from Karvatchar city, the natural hot spring Jermajur is located. The temperature of the water is 60ºC regardless the season. The stream of the water reaches 7m. There is a basin/pool built around the spring to swim in.

*"We Are Our Mountains",
the symbol of Karabakh*

Gandzasar

Gandzasar monastery is located on the hill opposite village Vank. It received its name from the hill, which is rich in silver and other metals. The name can be loosely translated from Armenian as "the treasure mountain". The cathedral and the atrium have survived. St. John the Baptist cathedral was built in 1216–1238 by Hasan Jalalyan, the prince of Nerkin Khachen. Its atrium (gavit) was constructed in 1266. The monastery is famous for being rich in various architectural ornaments. With regard to external decorations, the architect paid special attention to 16–edge dome, where one may find high ktitoric reliefs of Adam and Eva, Jesus Christ and Holy Mother of God. The Western entrance of the atrium is delicately cut. Below the altar of the cathedral there is the buried head of St. John the Baptist, which was brought from Venice by the Armenian traders. The monastery served as a center of education and a library, where diverse manuscripts were written. In the XVIII century the monastery was converted into a center of liberation movement and maintained its role until 1815 when the bishopric was transferred to Shushi. After Karabakh war the monastery was restored thanks to the support of the philanthropist L.Hayrapetyan.

Tigranakert

Tigranakert of Artsakh is situated in Askeran region of the Republic of Artsakh at the south-eastern foot of Vankasar mount, which is located in the lower valley of the river Khachenaget. The city was founded by the Armenian king Tigranes the Second (95-55 B.C.) at the end of the 90s B.C. and occupied the area of 70 ha. The traces of the city were first discovered in 2005 by the Artsakh Archeological Expedition of the Institute of Archaeology and Ethnography of NAS RA (leader H. Petrosyan). The upper part of the ancient Fortified Quarter of the citadel and the retaining fortress wall, which separated the Citadel from the Fortified Quarter, were opened during the excavations, moreover, the base of the southern walls of the fortress, which was cut into the rock and was approximately 450 m long, a section of northern wall of the fortress more than 272 m long and 5 m high, early medieval section with two churches, a crypt, the remnants of a monumental stele and an early Christian necropolis were found during the excavation process. The first antique quarter and the winery again cut into the rock were also uncovered and excavated. Excavations also took place in the area of ancient necropolis. There is a church on the top of Mount Vankasar, constructed in the 7 century, and approximately 3, 3 km from Tigranakert, on the northern edge of the cliff-an early Christian cult-cave complex and a water canal. There are also cross compositions with Greek and Armenian inscriptions in the territory of the complex.

Dadivank

According to the tradition, the monastery was founded at the site where Dadi, one of the disciples of apostle Thaddeus, had fallen as a martyr. St. Katoghike church of Dadivank monastery was constructed in 1214 by the princess of Aterk Arzu Khatun in memory of her late husband Prince Vaghtang and two sons. In 1921 during the Sovietization process, Nagorno Karabagh was handed over to Bolshevik Azerbaijan. Dadivank monastery was neglected, even worse, was made into a stable. And only in 1993 when the territory was liberated it faced its revival.

In 2014-2015 the specialists from Italy – architect-restorer, doctor Ara Zaryan and wall painting restoration specialist, doctor Christian Lamure, restored the wall paintings (XIII c.) preserved on the southern and northern walls of St. Katoghike church. Dadivank monastery's wall paintings are noteworthy because of their theme: one of them depicts the scene of the enthronement of St. Nicholas, the other shows St. Stephen's martyrdom. The narthex (its front wall represents and arcade) was constructed to the western wall of the main church in 1241. The church of St. Gregory which served for many centuries as a mausoleum for the princes of Verin Khachen is situated to the east of the main church. This grand monastic complex is one of the most important cultural centers.

Ghazanchetsots

St. Savour of Ghazanchetsots church (1886), being the pride of Shushi, is situated right in the city center. On the west side of the church there is a three–story bell tower, where one may encounter four sculptures of angels playing bugles. Those are copies, since the original ones were destroyed during Karabakh war. The church is comprised of a hall (34.7 x 23 x 35m) with a center dome supported by four central pillars. The stone used during the construction is lime. After 1920 massacres the cathedral stopped functioning. During the Soviet times it served as a granary, afterwards as a garage; during Karabakh war it was an Azeri deposit for the "Grad" system missiles. The cathedral was entirely reconstructed and since 1998 has been functioning again.

Shushi

Shushi fortress was built in the XVIII century and belonged to the prince Melik–Shakhnazaryan. Later he gave it to khan Panakh Ali. The walls of the fortress stretch around

2.5km getting mixed with the natural rock that with its steep cliffs goes down the gorge and climbs back again uniting with the wall. The walls are made of lime. They had 7–8m in height and were enhanced with semi–circular towers.

For this very fortress-city on 8-9 May 1992 one of the toughest battles of Karabakh war erupted. On 8 May, the Armenian tanks surrounded Shushi, occupied by the Azeri, and on 9 May the assault terminated with the victory of the Armenian troops. The current city is under restoration with the support of Pan–Armenian "Hayastan" fund.

Askeran (Mayraberd)

In the middle ages there used to be a fortress and an Armenian settlement in this place which was called Mayraberd. In the XVIII century a new powerful fortress, fortified with double walls, was constructed on approaches to Shushi to protect it. The fortress is situated in the southern outskirts of Askeran on both banks of the river Karkar on the way to Aghdam. It is 16-17 km north-east of Stepanakert. The walls of the fortress are 2 m wide and 9 m high. There are circular towers in the walls which are made of small pebbles and limestone with the help of mortar. The towers functioned as observation posts. The walls used to have narrow corridors serving as communication between the towers.

Amaras

According to the Armenian historian of the V century Pavstos Byuzand, the monastery was founded by St. Gregory the Illuminator in the IV century. It is also known that the grandson of St. Gregory the Illuminator, Grigoris, was buried in the eastern part of the church. He was the first bishop of Diocese of Artsakh. Another interesting fact is that Mesrop Mashtots (the creator of the Armenian alphabet) established the first school of Artsakh exactly here which gave a boost to the dissemination of the Armenian script in this region. In the Middle Ages Amaras monastery was the cultural and spiritual center of Artsakh while during the Soviet period of time it was abandoned. It was reopened in 1992 and is now an active monastery of Diocese of Artsakh.

Plane tree in Skhtorashen

Near the village of Skhtorashen the biggest plane tree in the territory of the former USSR is located. It is more than 2 thousand–year–old and rises up to 54m in height. The

diameter of the basis of the trunk is 27m. The tree has a hollow with the area of 44m², which can easily fit up to ten people. The leaves of the tree are measured to be more than half a meter.

Umbrellas (Mamrot kar)

The waterfall "Umbrellas" is a rock formation totally covered with moss where water drops and flows, this is where the second name of the waterfall, Mamrot Kar which literally means a stone covered with moss, comes from. This is an incredible place situated in the gorge of the Unot, under Jdrduz (Katarota). When you look from above, it seems that it is impossible to go down to the gorge. However, there is a very simple route to the Unot gorge - a walking trail from the village of Mkhitarashen near Shushi.

Yerevan

Yerevan is the capital of the Republic of Armenia. It extends from the central part Ararat valley, from the plain to the slopes, that rise to the North and give an "amphitheat shape to the city. The maximum altitude reaches 1400m in the North and 860m in the Sou The city is situated on the bank of the river Hrazdan.

The history of the city dates back to the Urartian Erebuni fortress constructed in 782 BC king Argishti I, which implies that Yerevan is 29 years older than Rome and it is one of most ancient cities in the world. The ruins of the fortress, that nowadays are part of Ereb museum, are located in the eastern part of the city.

The original cuneiform inscription left by the Urartian king about the construction of the c can be found there. This inscription is considered to be the "passport" of the city. Yerev was the capital of the first Republic of Armenia (1918). On 4 December 1920 it was occup by the Red Army and continued to be the capital of the Soviet Socialist Republic of Armen one of the fifteen republics of the Soviet Union. The country accepted the Bolsheviks' pov The Soviet era transformed the city into a modern industrial metropolis with more than c million inhabitants, reconstructed in accordance with the project of the prominent Armen architect Alexander Tamanyan starting from 1924.

He developed a specific national style using the elements of church architecture and tufa, a construction material. As a result of the reconstruction, the city completely altered; almost

the buildings that had been built earlier were demolished. Tamanian's most important piece is the Opera and Ballet building, the project that won a Grand Prix in Paris in 1937. The project itself was implemented afterwards. The construction of the Cascade complex is also one of his ideas, carried out by Armenian architects after his death (J. Torosyan, S. Gurzadyan, A. Mkhitaryan). It is a system of stairs with fountains and monuments on each floor.

The system harmonically connects the city center to the district of Kanaker, located on the hills. There are various exhibition halls inside the Cascade. Five platforms have been built (the sixth one is under construction). Each platform has its own fountains, sculptures; one may use the stairs outside or the internal escalator to go up the Cascade.

On the territory of the Cascade diverse sculptures from Cafesjian's collection are exhibited as well. The Northern Avenue is another of Tamanian's projects that was implemented not long ago (many buildings are still under construction). It is a pedestrian avenue, which stretches from the Opera House to the Republic Square.

The construction of the Square lasted from 1924 to 1958. It is comprised of five buildings: the History Museum, Government House with a tower and the main clock of the country, the Central Post Office. The National Gallery of Art can be found within the building of the History Museum. The gallery has three sections: Armenian, European and Russian. In the Armenian section the works of founders of Armenian laic paintings Hovnatanyan, those of the famous marine artist Ayvazovsky, Surenyants, Shahin, Kodjoyan, Saryan, Terlemezyan are exhibited.

Memorial to the victims of Genocide

Matenadaran (1957, architect Grigoryan) occupies a central place on the main avenue of the city, Mashtots Avenue, named after the inventor of the Armenian alphabet, Mesrop Mashtots. In front Matenadaran (1957, architect Grigoryan) is decorated with the monument of Mashtots, his students Koryun and the Armenian alphabet carved in stone. Mashtots is the creator of the Armenian alphabet (405) and probably the most prominent figure in the Armenian culture. Mashtots created 36 letters that are used till today (together with three more letters added in the XII century).

There are 17000 manuscripts (14000 are in Armenian) in Matenadaran. One can find the works of the greatest Armenian miniaturists Toros Roslin (XIII century, Cilicia) and Pitsak (XIV century, Cilicia) in the exhibition hall of the repository. Additionally, Matenadaran possesses the first Armenian translation of the Bible, works of medieval Armenian scientists, mathematics piece of Anania Shirakatsi (VII century), medicine–related documents of Mkhitar Heratsi (XII century), works of various historians, cartographs and alike.

On the high hill behind Matenadaran rises the magnificent monument of Mother Armenia (architect Harutyunyan), victoriously overlooking at the city. It was placed there in 1967 instead of Stalin's statue.

Opera House

From France Square, which is just in front of the Opera House, Sayat Nova and Baghramyan avenues proceed. The buildings of the National Assembly (1948–1950, architect Grigoryan), Presidential Residence (1951–1953, architect Grigoryan) and National Academy of Science (1955) are situated in Baghramyan Street. The house museum of the greatest Armenian composer Aram Khachaturyan, the author of ballets Gayane and Spartak, is also situated on the same street. On Sayat Nova Street one can find Saint Katoghike church (XIII century), one of the most ancient churches of the capital. The memorial dedicated to the victims of Genocide is located in Tsitsernakaberd Park. It was constructed in 1965–1967. Armenian Genocide Museum–Institute, inaugurated in 1995, can be found in the same area.

In Tigran Mets avenue, not far from the Republic Square, the cathedral of Saint Gregory the Illuminator was constructed in 2001 (architect Kyurkchyan) dedicated to the 1700th anniversary since Armenia officially adopted Christianity. The building was constructed with the support of various donors (Manukyan, Ghazaryan, Gevorgyan, Eurnekyan).

The only mosque preserved in the city is the Blue Mosque (1765), which is located in Mashtots avenue. The contemporary Yerevan is quite a safe and secure city. It has a very lively atmosphere, especially during summer and autumn seasons. It offers a plethora of cultural events and activities, has a number of concert halls, theatres, cinemas and clubs.

Cascade

Abovyan St., Yerevan

Gastronomy

The Armenian cuisine is one of the most ancient cuisines in Asia and the oldest one in Transcaucasia. Its characteristic features have been shaped over millennia, and most importantly, they are still being kept. The most essential thing is to use the old technique of preparing food in "thonir", a vertical oven, and to serve it in clay plates. The preparation technology is quite hard and demanding; the great quantity of dishes of meat, fish and vegetables is based on stuffing and the preparation of puré type mixtures.

Since the immemorial times the existence of agriculture in the valley of Ararat allowed the utilization of a great amount of vegetables and cereals. The principal product that occupies an extremely important role in the Armenian cuisine is "lavash": soft, thin flatbread prepared in a vertical oven. The next important product is cheese, offered in a very rich and tasty variety. Herbs and fruits also play a relevant role. Another peculiar feature is seasoning meat and fish dishes with various spices: coriander, dill, fennel, mint, pepper, tarragon, basil, garlic; for deserts cinnamon, cardamom, saffron and vanilla are often used.

It is worth mentioning that the Armenian cuisine, due to big Armenian Diaspora, has incorporated a lot of dishes from abroad as well (especially from Asia).

Several Armenian dishes

Harisa:　　　an almost homogenous mass made of wheat, chicken and butter.

Dolma:　　　minced meat (usually beef) mixed with rice and wrapped into grape leaves or cabbage

Ishli Kyufta:　veal, mixed with bulghur (ground coarse wheat) stuffed with minced meat (sometimes with walnuts)

Chaloma:　　Tortilla with basturma (Armenian dried sausage, beef)

Aylazan:　　a soup made of eggplants, potatoes, onions, green beans, tomatoes, oil (in Armenian cuisine mostly sunflower oil is used)

Khashlama:　beef or lamb, potatoes, tomatoes, carrot, onion

Khorovats:　pork, beef, lamb or fish first seasoned and grilled afterwards

Spas:　　　a soup made of matsun (the Armenian natural yoghurt) and wheat

Desserts

Gata:　　　　　puff pastry with "khoriz" (filling made of butter and sugar, sometimes with walnuts and almonds)

Baklava Armenia:　puff pastry filled with walnuts (or peanuts), honey and cinnamon

Drinks

Tan — Matsun (yoghurt) with water and salt

Wine — Armenian wine

Brandy — Armenian brandy is known all over the world

The food is not spicy: however, quite a lot of salt is used in the Armenian cuisine.

Parables

The lazy daughter–in–law

There was a couple living in a village. They had only one son and as they were already rather old, it was extremely difficult for them to do the housework, bring water, clean the house and prepare bread. One day they decided to marry their son.

— Let's marry our son,— said the old man to his wife,— we are already old and can't do the housework ourselves anymore.

The son got married and the daughter–in–law came to their house. One week passed after the other. One month passed but the daughter–in–law was not doing anything in the house. Just like before, the parents–in–law continued doing the whole job, while the daughter–in–law spent her days eating or lying on the carpet. The old people started thinking how to make the girl work.

— Look,— said the mother–in–law,— let's go to the garden and begin arguing on who should get water today. The daughter–in–law will hear our discussion; she will be ashamed, will get up and go for for water herself. They acted according to their plan. The couple went to the garden and started arguing. And the man told his wife;

— It is your turn to bring water today.

The woman shouted at her husband; And the man told his wife;

— No, it is your turn today.

Hearing the discussion, the daughter–in–law appeared in the garden;

— Father, why are you arguing? You can fetch water today and you, mother, can bring it tomorrow,—said the girl calmly, entered the house, closed the door and sat on the carpet.

The king

The bad and lazy child was very often told,

— Ay, ay, you'll never become human being.

Years passed and the bad and lazy child became a king, no more, no less.

He returned to his village and said;

— Have you seen that I'm a king now?And you were telling me……

The neighbors replied to him;

— We never told you that you would not be a king. We have always told you that you would never be a human being.

Legends

The legend of lavash

During the ancient times there was a king in Armenia, whose name was Aram. During one of the battles the king Aram was captured by the Assyrian ruler Nosor. The winner put down a condition for the Armenian king.

— You will spend ten days without eating anything. Then, on the 11th day, you and I will have an archery competition. In case you win, I will let you go safe and sound to your country with presents that worth the king.

The following day Aram asked to bring him the most beautiful shield from the Armenian army. The latter was at the border of Assyria. The Assyrian messengers began their route to the Armenian camp. The Armenians immediately understood that by asking for the shield their king was trying to give them a sign. In order to win some time, they kept the messengers there for the whole night.

At dawn the messengers finally brought the shield requested by the king Aram. Nobody knew that very delicate bread was hidden inside the shield since none of the Assyrians ever heard of lavash; whom would it occur to look for bread within a shield to?

The king Aram received the shield but the following day he suddenly declared that this shield was not the one he required. What could be done? The messengers were once again sent to the border to get the new shield. However, this was also not the one that the king wanted. In this manner, ten days in a row the king was asking for a new shield and the messengers were crossing the same distance again and again, bringing him lavash without even suspecting it.

On the eleventh day Aram and Nosor went to the shooting field. Nosor was convinced that Aram, being left without food for 10 days, lost his power, spirit and his vision got weak. But what a miracle! Aram was the winner of the competition and returned to his country with honor. The Armenian bread lavash saved his life. Returning to his homeland, the king ordered everyone to only prepare lavash in the whole territory of Armenia ever since.

The legend of duduk

Once upon a time, wandering around the world, the Young Wind met a beautiful Tree. He had never seen anything like her. He was delighted with the Tree. Softly blowing on the delicate petals of her flowers, barely touching her leaves he sang sweet melodies that were heard in the whole surrounding.

When the Supreme Wind found out about the love of the Young Wind, he got terribly enraged. He came storming down from the top of the mountain destroying almost all plants on the Earth. The Young Wind hugged his lovely Tree, protecting her with all his power and told the Supreme Wind that he was ready to make any sacrifice, so that he could stay with his Tree.
— In that case you may stay. But keep in mind that from now on you will not be able to fly anymore,— answered the Supreme Wind.
The happy Young Wind wanted to return his wings but the Sir suddenly stopped him;
— No,— he said,— It would be too easy. I will give you a different punishment. I will leave you the wings. But as soon as you fly, your favorite Tree will die.
The Young Wind was satisfied. After all, he still had both: his love and his wings.
Everything was fabulous, but when the autumn came, the Tree lost all her leaves. The Young Wind no longer had the flowers or leaves to play with. He became very anxious.
Nearby his brothers were flying, dancing with the last leaves of the trees, filling the mountains with their victorious howl. It seemed they were calling for him to join them in their merry–go–round. One day, not being able to resist, the Young Wind left the ground and flew towards his brothers. At that very moment the Tree died. In one of its branches a small piece of Wind was left.
One day a child, who was gathering firewood, found the branch and made a flute (duduk) out of it. From the slightest touch of lips the instrument spreads a sad melody of separation all around.

Vardavar

The descendants of the Titan resented the village of Ario Man. Many times they invaded Ararat, but always encountered solid resistance. Among them was a very astute Hresh (Monster) and once he asked the God Vishap (Dragon) to take his troops to Ararat but Vishap rejected;
— Vahagn is in Ararat and I can't defeat him. Go to the Underworld God Yahweh. He is wise and shrewd. If he defeats Vahagn, I'll assist you in taking over the Arios.
The titan Hresh made many sacrifices to God Yahweh. In the end Yahweh appeared before him;
— Your admiration is surprising and it deserves a prize. Tell me what you need.
— I want Ararat. I want my nation and not the Arios to live there.
— The Charios living there will not become Arios; don't dare to go against the laws of the Creature. You will lose.

— But I have to take revenge. Moreover, you also resent Vahagn. Help me to conquer Ararat and I'll sacrifice many things to you.

— You ask too much of me. But be aware that your power is in the weakness of the Arios. The power of the Arios is in Vahagn and the source of power of Vahagn is Love. If there is no more love among the Arios, Vahagn will not be able to protect them. The Sun will set in Ararat, the Arios will remain without any power and you will be able to take over their land with the support of Vishap.

— And who will be able to destroy Love among the Arios?

— Only me. I'll steal Love, hide her in my underground kingdom, but I need power to do it; if your nation believes in me, I'll be the most powerful one.

Hresh accepted the conditions and his nation started adoring Yahweh. The Underworld God gained power quickly. He started persecuting the Goddess of Love, Astghik.

One day when Astghik, unaware of the plot, was having a bath in the river Yeraskh, Yahweh attacked her, kidnapped her and took her to his underground kingdom. The Arios were confused; Love disappeared from Ararat. They searched everywhere for her but she was nowhere to be found.

Yahweh was enjoying the difficult times of the Arios: "You will never find your Love but I will give you another love; love towards hatred and death". You will hate yourselves and your God Vahagn".

Yahweh used all his anger and shed it all over Ararat. Ararat trembled, the land tottered and it exploded throwing out fire and burning lava. Palaces and temples collapsed, entire cities were destroyed burying many Arios under their ruins. Those who survived were in panic; the thick smoke was hurting both their eyes and their souls. The faces of the Arios became very sad; their looks were full of grief. The terror and fury reigned all around. Arios started hating each other, hating the song and the smile, Ararat and the Sun. They gathered all their terror, all their wrath and directed it to the sky. The sun faded away, flowers and plants withered, rivers and streams dried out, birds abandoned Ararat.

And with the help of Vishap Hresh got established in the land of Ararat.

Instead of love towards life, love towards death and hatred filled the hearts of the Arios. The smiles disappeared; no songs were heard. Wives were leaving their husbands, parents were giving up on their children, and brothers were fighting against their siblings.

The Titans of the Charios were delighted and were sacrificing Arios to Yahweh.

The powerful Vahagn was worried;

— Father,— told Ara,— I'm the Head of the Cosmic Power. Can't I save my Ario nation from this humiliating slavery?

— No,— said the father,— you can't save them before they ask for it. The strength of your power is Love. Find Astghik, return Love towards the Sun to Arios and then they will call you and you'll regain your Power.

Vahagn was looking for Astghik everywhere but was unable to find her; he could not hear her voice. Yahweh, after finding out that Vahagn was searching for her, made destructions with Charios' hands, so that Vahagn did not hear her; Astghik's voice would get lost in constant crying, howling and pleas of the people.

Vahagn told the Mother Goddess, Anahit;

— How can I hear Astghik's voice in this incredible noise?

— Find a child in Ararat,— replied the Mother,— who has not experienced hatred yet; whose eyes are still full of fire for life, whose soul has not yet lost the desire to live. He will be able to hear the voice of Astghik.

In the mountains of Ararat Vahagn saw a tired, exhausted child, who was tripping and falling while moving.

— Child,— Vahagn asked him,— who are you and where are you going so tired?

— I'm looking for Vahagn, because I've heard Astghik's voice calling for him. If Vahagn liberates her, my parents will start loving me again.

He led Vahagn to the rock, where he heard Astghik's voice. Vahagn shouted;

–Yahweh, I've arrived. Give me back Astghik or come out to fight with me.

But Yahweh did not show up for the battle; he got frightened and retreated farther inside his kingdom.

With his Lightning Sword Vahagn hit the rock. It shattered and a hole appeared from where Vahagn saved Astghik.

Astghik flew to the sky, received the blessing of Father Ara and Mother Anahit, took a jar with blessed water and back to the Earth. She did not recognize Ararat; there were only thorns, bones and vipers around. The vipers rushed away, and the people were looking at Astghik with astonishment. Astghik was giving roses to each of them and sprinkling the divine water from her jar. People changed, wounds got healed. They were looking at each other and smiling.

— Who are you,— they asked Astghik.

— I'm Astghik, the Goddess of Love. I'm giving you the divine Love back. We will cross the whole valley of Ararat singing and dancing, celebrating the holiday of Vardavar. We will give light to Arios with water and roses, so that they start smiling and loving again..

Parents and children were smiling, kids and youth were all happy. They loved each other and adored Astghik. Finally, the smile of Love started blossoming all over the valley of Ararat.

It was Vardavar: the holiday of Love.

Note: Nowadays, this holiday is still celebrated 98 days after Easter.

USEFUL INFORMATION

Yerevan Museums

FOLK ART MUSEUM
64 Abovyan str., tel.569383, 569387

DERENIK DEMIRCHYAN HOUSE-MUSEUM
29/4 Abovyan str., tel. 527774

MINAS AVETISYAN MEMORIAL MUSEUM
29 Nalbandyan str., tel. 560787

SPENDIARYAN HOUSE MUSEUM
21 Nalbandyan str, tel. 580783, 521299

MARTIROS SARYAN HOUSE MUSEUM
3 Saryan str., tel. 581762, 521607

NATIONAL GALLERY OF ARMENIA
1 Arami str., tel. 580812, 580816

EREBUNI MUSEUM
38 Erebuni str, tel. 458207

KHACHATUR ABOVYAN HOUSE MUSEUM
4 Kanakeri, 2nd str., tel. 284686

LITERATURE AND ART MUSEUM NAMED
AFTER YEGHISHE CHARENTS
1 Arami str., tel. 563641 581651

YERVAND KOCHAR MUSEUM
39/12 Mashtotsi ave., tel. 580612, 529326

HOVHANNES TUMANYAN MUSEUM
40 Moskovyan str., tel. 560021, 581271

AVETIK ISAHAKYAN HOUSE MUSEUM
76 Baghramyan str., tel. 562424, 587380

ARAM KHACHATRYAN HOUSE-MUSEUM
3 Zarubian str., tel. 580178, 589418

SERGEY PARAJANOW MUSEUM
15/16 Dzorapi str., tel. 538473

MODERN ART MUSEUM
7 Mashtots ave., tel. 535359, 535567

YEREVAN HISTORY MUSEUM
1/1 Argishti str., tel. 568109

CHILDREN'S ART GALLERY
13 Abovyan str., tel. 520951

YEGHISHE CHARENTS HOUSE-MUSEUM
17 Mashtots str., tel. 535594, 531412

RUSSIAN ART MUSEUM (COLLECTION OF
PROFESSOR A.ABRAHAMYAN)
38 Isahakyan str., tel. 560872,560331

STATE MUSEUM OF NATURE OF ARMENIA
36 Tigran Mets ave., tel. 567791 527942

MUSEUM-INSTITUTE OF THE ARMENIAN
GENOCIDE
Tsitsernakaberd Park, tel. 390981, 391414

MATENADARAN RESEARCH INSTITUTE OF
ANCIENT MANUSCRIPTS AFTER MASH-
TOTS
53 Mashtots str., tel. 583292 562578 520420

MAYR HAYASTAN WAR MUSEUM, MINIS-
TRY OF DEFENCE OF ARMENIA
2 Azatutyan str., tel. 251400

CAFESJIAN MUSEUM FOUNDATION
Cascade Complex, tel. 541932, 541934

HISTORY MUSEUM OF ARMENIA
Republic Square, tel. 582761, 565322

NATIONAL MUSEUM-INSTITUTE OF
ARCHITECTURE
Government House, tel. 251400

MUSEUM OF WOODCARVING
2 and 4 Paronyan str., tel. 532461

MIDDLE EAST MUSEUM
1 Arami str., tel. 567791 527942

Artbridge bookstore-cafe
20 Abovyan str., Yerevan, Armenia
+374 10 521 239, +374 10 581 284
artbridge1@gmail.com
artbridge.am

Art Boutique

KARA
ART IN SILVER

Wonder'em all
and wonder yourself

0002, Yerevan, 54 Pushkin str.
(+37410) 53 65 25, www.kara.am

ZANGAK
BOOKSTORE

Bookstore and cultural center "Zangak", 7 Abovyan street,
Yerevan, E-mail: info@zangak.am, tel.: +374 11 22 33 66

The Guidebook of
ARMENIA

NATURE, HISTORY, CULTURE, RELIGION

Fourth edition, expanded

Collected by *Zaruhi Orbelyan*
Editor of historical material: *Ruben Hovsepyan (PhD in History)*
Translated by *Naira Harutyunyan*
Redacted by *Anna Tumasyan*
Designer: *Jack Topalakyan*
Cartographers: *Grig Beglaryan, Anushavan Barseghyan*

Bibliography:
1. "The History of Armenia", textbooks (Yerevan, 1998, in Armenian)
2. "Armenia" guidebook for pilgrims and tourists (Yerevan 1998, in Armenian)
3. "Armenian Brief Encyclopedia" (Yerevan 1990, in Armenian)
4. "Armenian Church", M. Ormanyan (Yerevan 2006, in Armenian)
5. "Armenia, travelers' encyclopedia" (Yerevan 1990, in Russian)